First World War
and Army of Occupation
War Diary
France, Belgium and Germany

36 DIVISION
Divisional Troops
Divisional Ammunition Column
21 September 1915 - 28 February 1919

WO95/2496/8

The Naval & Military Press Ltd
www.nmarchive.com
Published in association with The National Archives

Published by

The Naval & Military Press Ltd

Unit 10 Ridgewood Industrial Park,

Uckfield, East Sussex,

TN22 5QE England

Tel: +44 (0) 1825 749494

www.naval-military-press.com

www.nmarchive.com

This diary has been reprinted in facsimile from the original. Any imperfections are inevitably reproduced and the quality may fall short of modern type and cartographic standards.

© Crown Copyright
Images reproduced by permission of The National Archives, London, England, 2015.

Contents

Document type	Place/Title	Date From	Date To
Heading	WO95/2496/8		
Heading	36th Division Divl Ammn Column Sep 1915-Feb 1919		
Heading	36th Division 10th Divl: A.C. (36th Division) Vol I Oct 15-Feb 19		
Heading	War Diary of Divisional Ammunition Column. From 1st To 31st Oct 1915		
War Diary	Southampton	05/10/1915	05/10/1915
War Diary	Havre	06/10/1915	07/10/1915
War Diary	Longeau	07/10/1915	07/10/1915
War Diary	Breilly Sur Somme	07/10/1915	07/10/1915
War Diary	Canaples	22/10/1915	22/10/1915
War Diary	Bordon	05/10/1915	05/10/1915
War Diary	Greenham Common Newbury	21/09/1915	21/09/1915
War Diary	Basingstoke	21/09/1915	22/09/1915
War Diary	Bordon	22/09/1915	29/09/1915
War Diary	Bordon	05/10/1915	05/10/1915
Heading	War Diary of 10th Divisional Ammn Column (attached 36th Divn) From 1st Nov 1915 To 30th Nov 1915 Vol II		
Miscellaneous	36th D.A.C.	25/02/1916	25/02/1916
War Diary	Canaples	27/11/1915	28/11/1915
War Diary		02/11/1915	17/11/1915
War Diary	Bernaville	17/11/1915	21/11/1915
War Diary	Canaples	22/11/1915	23/11/1915
War Diary	Bernaville	25/11/1915	25/11/1915
War Diary	Fransu	28/11/1915	28/11/1915
Heading	36th D.A.C. Vol I II III		
War Diary	Bordon	27/11/1915	27/11/1915
War Diary	Havre	28/11/1915	30/11/1915
War Diary	Villers Sous Ailly	06/12/1915	09/12/1915
War Diary	Le Toile	23/12/1915	05/01/1916
War Diary	Canaples Halloy	10/01/1916	10/01/1916
War Diary	St. Ouen	11/01/1916	11/01/1916
War Diary	Canaples	12/01/1916	12/01/1916
War Diary	St Ouen	19/01/1916	01/02/1916
War Diary	Puchevillers	01/02/1916	01/02/1916
War Diary	St Ouen	03/02/1916	24/02/1916
War Diary	La Vicogne	25/02/1916	25/02/1916
Heading	36 Div Ac Vol 5		
Heading	173rd Bde: Rfa Vol : 4		
Heading	36th D.A.C. Vol: IV		
War Diary	La Vicogne	01/03/1916	01/03/1916
War Diary	Arqueves	03/03/1916	03/03/1916
War Diary	Belle Eglise	03/03/1916	03/03/1916
War Diary	Arqueves	04/03/1916	31/03/1916
War Diary	Puchevillers	09/04/1916	20/06/1916
War Diary	Hedauville	28/06/1916	29/06/1916
War Diary	Hedauville Wood	01/07/1916	03/07/1916
War Diary	Varennes	05/07/1916	14/07/1916
War Diary	On Line Of March	15/07/1916	18/07/1916

War Diary	Tournehem	19/07/1916	20/07/1916
War Diary	Line of March	21/07/1916	22/07/1916
War Diary	E. of Bailleul	24/07/1916	31/01/1917
War Diary	In The Field E of Bailleul	14/02/1917	25/02/1917
War Diary	N.E. Of Bailleul	28/03/1917	31/05/1917
Heading	Bm		
War Diary	N.E. Bailleul	01/06/1917	25/06/1917
War Diary	Dranoutre	26/06/1917	08/07/1917
War Diary	W. Of Poperinghe	09/07/1917	24/07/1917
War Diary	E of Poperinghe	25/07/1917	31/07/1917
War Diary	East of Vlamentinghe	15/08/1917	29/08/1917
War Diary	Le Mesnil	30/08/1917	03/09/1917
War Diary	Equancourt	04/09/1917	05/11/1917
War Diary	Barastre	06/11/1917	14/11/1917
War Diary	Haplincourt	15/11/1917	19/11/1917
War Diary	Ruyaulcourt	20/11/1917	12/12/1917
War Diary	Ytres	13/12/1917	26/12/1917
War Diary	Beaulencourt	27/12/1917	02/01/1918
War Diary	Vaire	03/01/1918	07/01/1918
War Diary	Hangest	08/01/1918	13/01/1918
War Diary	Dury	14/01/1918	17/01/1918
War Diary	St Simon	17/01/1918	28/02/1918
Heading	36th Divisional Artillery. 36th Divisional Ammunition Column R.F.A. March 1918		
War Diary	St Simon	01/03/1918	21/03/1918
War Diary	Somette Eaucourt	21/03/1918	21/03/1918
War Diary	Verlaines	21/03/1918	21/03/1918
War Diary	Fretoy Le Chateau	22/03/1918	23/03/1918
War Diary	Avricourt.	23/03/1918	24/03/1918
War Diary	Fresnieres	25/03/1918	25/03/1918
War Diary	Orvillers	26/03/1918	26/03/1918
War Diary	Mery	27/03/1918	27/03/1918
War Diary	Gournay	28/03/1918	29/03/1918
War Diary	Grand Fresnoy	30/03/1918	30/03/1918
War Diary	La Rue St Pierre	31/03/1918	31/03/1918
Heading	36th Divisional Artillery. 36th Divisional Ammunition Column R.F.A. April 1918		
War Diary	La Rue St Pierre	01/04/1918	01/04/1918
War Diary	Auchy-La-Montagne	02/04/1918	02/04/1918
War Diary	Charney	03/04/1918	07/04/1918
War Diary	Courselles	08/04/1918	10/04/1918
War Diary	Pont De Metz	11/04/1918	14/04/1918
War Diary	Hopoutre	15/04/1918	15/04/1918
War Diary	Mont Des Cats	16/04/1918	16/04/1918
War Diary	Godewaersvelde	17/04/1918	24/04/1918
War Diary	Hamhoek	24/04/1918	24/04/1918
War Diary	Peselhoek	25/04/1918	11/05/1918
War Diary	Hamhoek	12/05/1918	07/06/1918
War Diary	Pontypool Camp	08/06/1918	04/07/1918
War Diary	Zermezeele	05/07/1918	07/07/1918
War Diary	St Sylvestre Cappel	08/07/1918	10/07/1918
War Diary	Eecke	11/07/1918	31/08/1918
War Diary	Godewaersvelde	01/09/1918	02/09/1918
War Diary	Schaexken	02/09/1918	13/09/1918
War Diary	St Jans Cappel	14/09/1918	22/09/1918
War Diary	Wormhoudt	23/09/1918	27/09/1918

War Diary	St Jan Ter Biezen	28/09/1918	29/09/1918
War Diary	Vlamertinghe	30/09/1918	30/09/1918
Heading	26th War Bty.		
War Diary	Vlamertinghe	01/10/1918	03/10/1918
War Diary	Ypres.	04/10/1918	14/10/1918
War Diary	Dadizeele	15/10/1918	18/10/1918
War Diary	Lendeleede	18/10/1918	25/10/1918
War Diary	Bevern	26/10/1918	27/10/1918
War Diary	Lauwe	28/10/1918	03/11/1918
War Diary	Marcke	04/11/1918	12/11/1918
War Diary	Tourcoing	13/11/1918	28/02/1919

WO 05/24696

36TH DIVISION

DIVL AMMN COLUMN
SEP ~~OCT~~ 1915-FEB 1919

36TH DIVISION

36th Division

10th Division A.C.
 attd.
(36th Division)

Vol I

Oct 15

121/7431

av a/p

CONFIDENTIAL

WAR DIARY

of

DIVISIONAL AMMUNITION COLUMN.

From 1st to 31st Oct 1915

Army Form C. 2118

3

WAR DIARY
or
INTELLIGENCE SUMMARY
(Erase heading not required.)

Place	Date	Hour	Summary of Events and Information	Remarks and references to Appendices
SOUTHAMPTON	5·10·15	4 p.m.	Left SOUTHAMPTON in S. ships CARDIGANSHIRE, City of CHESTER, & MANHATTAN.	
HAVRE	6·10·15	10 a.m.	Arrived at HAVRE after a very uneventful & calm crossing	
"	6·10·15	7.30 a.m.	Disembarkation commenced & finished at 10.80 a.m.	
"	6·10·15		Entraining commenced at 8.30 p.m. the last train load left HAVRE at 7.45 a.m. on the 7·10·15. 5 trainloads being used.	
"	7·10·15			
LONGEAU	7·10·15	5.15 p.m.	Head quarters & part of No 1 Section, being the last train load detrained while watering horses in the river AVRE, a tributary of the SOMME, near LONGEAU. Lieut Mungo John SMITH, of No 1 Section displayed great courage & gallantry. Although fully clothed & armed, he jumped into the river, & saved from drowning No 23230 Driver R. STALKER No 1. Section, who, while riding a mule, had got into deep water, owing to the quick shelving bed of the stream. The driver was fully clothed & had his rifle slung on his back & would undoubtedly have been drowned had Lieut Smith	

WAR DIARY or INTELLIGENCE SUMMARY

Army Form C. 2118

Smith not have come to his rescue. The mule was drowned & the rifle lost. The matter was reported to Head Quarters 36. Div. & the following reply received.

H.Qrs
36. Ulster Division.

I consider the conduct of this officer worthy of commendation

(Signed) R. J. ELKINGTON
Brig. Gen.
Commanding 36 Div. arty.

13.10.15.

Headquarters
36 Div. Artillery

The G.O.C. wishes to express to L/Smith his appreciation of the gallant conduct he displayed in undoubtedly saving the life of Driver STALKER on the 7th Oct. 1915.

(Signed) H.C. SINGLETON Major
DAA&QMS 36th Division

D.H.Q. 14.10.15

Army Form C. 2118

WAR DIARY
or
INTELLIGENCE SUMMARY
(Erase heading not required.)

Instructions regarding War Diaries and Intelligence Summaries are contained in F. S. Regs., Part II. and the Staff Manual respectively. Title Pages will be prepared in manuscript.

Place	Date	Hour	Summary of Events and Information	Remarks and references to Appendices
BREILLY SUR SOMME	7/10/15		In Billets from 7.10.15 until 22.10.15 at BREILLY-SUR-SOMME	
CANAPLES	22/10/15		Moved to new billets in CANAPLES 22-10-15 — 31.10.15	

WAR DIARY
or
INTELLIGENCE SUMMARY
(Erase heading not required.)

Army Form C. 2118

Place	Date	Hour	Summary of Events and Information	Remarks and references to Appendices
BORDON	5.10.15		Strength (including A.S.C attached) 11 officers 864 other ranks 734 horses 110, 4 wheeled vehicles, 3. 2wheeled vehicles, 5 bicycles. The following is a list of officers who proceeded overseas.	
			Lieut-Colonel William Horenden FOLLIOTT. Commanding	
			2nd Lieut. JOHN STRATTON STORRAR acting adjutant.	
			Lieut JOHN FINBAR HUNT. R.A.M.C.	
			Captain FRANCIS JOHN NEWTON DUNNE. Officer commanding No 1. Section	
			Lieut MUNGO JOHN SMITH No 1 Section	
			2nd Lieut JOHN WILLIAM DONALD FISHER No 1 Section.	
			2nd Lieut WILLIAM JAMES FENNELL Officer Commanding No 2 Section	
			2nd Lieut. JOHN BLUMER No 2 Section.	
			Captain FREDERICK ECKERSALL NIXON-ECKERSALL O.C. No 3 Section	
			2nd Lieut. JOHN EDMUND KELLY LYNAM. No 3 Section	
			2nd Lieut ANDREW McLAREN SPIERS No 3 Section	
			The following officer was left behind at BORDON in charge of Base Details	
			2nd Lieut F. O. TRECHMAN.	

Army Form C. 2118

X. Divisional Ammunition Column.

WAR DIARY
or
INTELLIGENCE SUMMARY
(Erase heading not required.)

Instructions regarding War Diaries and Intelligence Summaries are contained in F.S. Regs., Part II. and the Staff Manual respectively. Title Pages will be prepared in manuscript.

Place	Date	Hour	Summary of Events and Information	Remarks and references to Appendices
Greenham Common NEWBURY.	21.9.15		The X. Div. A.C. left NEWBURY for BORDON on the 21.9.15 to prepare for service in FRANCE with the 36th (Ulster) Division, under W.O. letter 121/6543 M. dated 17th Sep. 1915, to be mobilized on W.E. part VII. New Armies 1915 pages 56 to 63, with the addition of 3 wagons (G.S.) for 18pr ammunition, 6 drivers, & 12 draught horses.	
BASINGSTOKE	21.9.15 to 22.9.15		Bivouac at BASINGSTOKE on the night of the 21-22/9/15. Received 3 extra wagons (G.S.) from the 11th Div. A.C. - 9 drivers + 18 mules being substituted for the 6 drivers & 12 draught horses. The 11th Div. A.C. having only mules on their establishment.	
BORDON.	22.9.15.		Arrived at BORDON from BASINGSTOKE, & occupied part of GUADALUPE Barracks.	
"	24.9.15		2nd Lieut. & a/ adjutant J. R. JONES was badly kicked by a mule & his arm fractured, & admitted to the CAMBRIDGE HOSPITAL, ALDERSHOT on 24.9.15.	
"	29.9.15		The X Div. A.C. were inspected (along with the 36th (Ulster) Division) by His Majesty the King on HANKLEY COMMON on the 29.9.15.	
"	5.10.15		Left BORDON for SOUTHAMPTON DOCKS (occupying 8 trains) first train leaving at 12.35 am, & last train at 8.30 am on 5.10.15.	

Vol II

Confidential

War Diary

of

~~Head Qrs~~
10th Divisional Ammn Column
(attached 36th Divn)

from 1st Nov 1915 to 30th Nov 1915

Vol II

~~36th~~

~~12th D.A.C. (12th)~~

	Oct	
Vol I	3.11.15	17.11.15
Vol II	Nov.	
Vol III	Dec. 30.1.16	2.2.16
Vol 4	Jan. 4.2.16	6.2.16

to 56th

~~12th D.A.C.~~ (note 10)

25.2.16

Army Form C. 2118

WAR DIARY
INTELLIGENCE SUMMARY
(Erase heading not required.)

X Divisional Ammunition Column

Place	Date	Hour	Summary of Events and Information	Remarks and references to Appendices
CANAPLES	22/10/15 till 28/11/15		In billets at CANAPLES from 22/10/15 until 28/11/15	
	2.11.15		Reported horse lines are in very bad condition owing to wet weather	
	6.11.15		moved horse lines to new standings	
	6.11.15		continual complaints were made from 17.10.15 until 6.11.15 as to shortages of rations & forage	
	12.11.15		Lieut E. SEE joined & posted to No 2 Section	
	13.11.15		Reported that horse lines are in very bad condition owing to constant wet weather, moved to fresh ground.	
	14.11.15		Reported difficulty experienced in getting a sufficient supply of nose bags.	
	14.11.15		Inspection by CRA & ADVS of horses.	
	15.11.15		Commenced to make horse standings	
	17.11.15		No 3 Section moved to BERNAVILLE on 17th to billets there	
BERNAVILLE	21.11.15		DDVS VII Corps. CRA & ADVS inspected horses at BERNAVILLE & CANAPLES.	
CANAPLES	22.11.15		Lieut W.D. CONNOCHIE. AVC. joined the Column as V.O. i/c.	
	23.11.15		Lieut SMITH & 2nd Lieut BLUMER. & 30 men 44 horses & 6 G.S. wagons are temporarily attached to 1/4 London Brigade R.F.A. & left to join on this date 23/11/15.	

Army Form C. 2118

WAR DIARY
INTELLIGENCE SUMMARY
(Erase heading not required.)

Instructions regarding War Diaries and Intelligence Summaries are contained in F. S. Regs., Part II. and the Staff Manual respectively. Title Pages will be prepared in manuscript.

Place	Date	Hour	Summary of Events and Information	Remarks and references to Appendices
BERNAVILLE	27/11/15		No 3 Section moved from BERNAVILLE to new billets at BONNEVILLE.	
FRANSU	28/11/15		The Column moved from CANAPLES & BONNEVILLE to new billets at FRANSU on 28.11.15.	

Army Form C.2118.

AMMUNITION COLUMN R.F.A.
No. C/182
Date 11-2-16

WAR DIARY
or
INTELLIGENCE SUMMARY

Ulster Div: Ammn. Col.

(Erase heading not required.)

Instructions regarding War Diaries and Intelligence Summaries are contained in F.S. Regs., Part II. and the Staff Manual respectively. Title Pages will be prepared in manuscript.

Place	Date	Hour	Summary of Events and Information	Remarks and references to Appendices
Gordon	27-11-15		The Column entrained in eight trains for Rouen	A.24
Havre	28-11-15		The Column disembarked at HAVRE with the exception of 1 officer 50 R.C. of Queen	A.24
—	29-30, 11-15		The Column entrained in five trains, detraining at PONT RÉMY and marched to VILLERS SOUS AILLY and went into Billets	A.24
VILLERS SOUS AILLY	6-12-15		The Remainder of Column joined up from HAVRE	A.24
—	9-12-15		The Column moved by road to L'ÉTOILE and went into Billets and were employed in construction of permanent Horse lines	A.24
L'ÉTOILE	23-12-15		Lieut. Fitzgerald and Lothian temporary attached and posted to HQ & Sections	A.24
—	28-12-15		Lieut. Lothian temporary attached and posted to No. 1 Section	A.24
—	28-12-15		Bt. Col. Thornton proceeded to England for dental treatment & Capt. Lee assumed command	A.24
—	31-12-15		Capt. W.C. Beck R.F.A. (T.F.) posted to England, Lieut. Julian assumed command Mr. Section	A.24
—	"		Lieut. Fitzgerald proceeded on Course of French Instr.	A.24
—	"		Lieut. Cookyes awarded 25 Brighton Casualty Clearing Station	A.24
—	4-1-16		Bt. Col. Thornton rejoined from England	A.24
—	5-1-16		The Column moved by road to CANAPLES and went into Billets with the exception of Column Head Quarter which billeted at HALLOY Les PERNOIS	A.24

WAR DIARY or INTELLIGENCE SUMMARY

Army Form C. 2118

Westn Div Ammn Col

Place	Date	Hour	Summary of Events and Information	Remarks and references to Appendices
CANAPLES NALLOY	10-1-16		Column Head Quarters and Nos 2 and 3 Sections moved by road and went into billets at ST OUEN	A.E.H
ST. OUEN	11-1-16		Major W. GRAHAM joined for duty from 108 Coys and assumed command of No. 2 Section	A.E.H
CAMAPLES	12-1-16		No 1 Section under Capt HEE moved by road and went into billets at PERNOIS	A.E.H
ST OUEN	19-1-16		No. 2 Section under Capt. LEE joined up with Column and went into Billets	A.E.H
	20-1-16		The following details of No. 3 Section moved by road to PUCHEVILLERS and went into billets and employed on transport duties for construction of railway lines:- Capt. J.R. NOBSON R.F.A., Lieut C.W.DYER R.F.A., Lieut C.W.DYER R.F.A., 45 Other ranks, 11 S. Horses and 9 G.S. Wagons	A.E.H
	29-1-16		The following details was sent to No 3 Section at PUCHEVILLERS: 30 Other Ranks, 36 Horses, 3 G.S. Wagons	A.E.H
	30-1-16		8 wagons under Lieut.'s J.B. PITT R.F.A. No. 2 Section proceeded to PROUVILLE & transport for 9 Royal Irish Fusiliers on the latter moving up to trenches	A.E.H
	" "		4 wagons of No. 2 Section under 2nd Lieut L.T.H HASKINS R.F.A. proceeded to BEAUMETZ and 9 wagons of No 3 Section under Lieut L.T.H HASKINS R.F.A. proceeded to RIBEAUCOURT on transport to 108 Infantry Brigade H.Q.	
	" "		duty in transport to 138 Royal Irish Rifles on the latter moving to trenches	A.E.H

1875 Wt. W593/826 1,000,000 4/15 J.B.C. & A. A.D.S.S./Forms/C. 2118.

Army Form C. 2118

Wales Div: Ammn Col

WAR DIARY
or
INTELLIGENCE SUMMARY
(Erase heading not required.)

Place	Date	Hour	Summary of Events and Information	Remarks and references to Appendices
ST OUEN	1.2.16		Major W. GRAHAM R.F.A. proceeded on leave to England. Lieut Julian assumed command of No 2 Section.	HPH
PUCHEVILLERS			The detachment of No 2 Section on command at PUCHEVILLERS.	HPH
ST OUEN	3.2.16		9 wagons No Section under Lieut B. CHESTER R.F.A. proceeded to BERNAVILLE moved to ARGUEVES for transport duty with 11th Royal Irish Rifles on latter moving to trenches.	HPH
"	5.2.16		8 wagons No 2 Section under Lieut d'Arcques R.F.A. proceeded to RIBEAUCOURT for transport duty with 12th Royal Irish Rifles on their latter moving to trenches.	HPH
"	6.2.16		8 Wagons under Lieut Pitt, attached 9 R.I. two having taken latter to MESNIL and H in wagon & S.O. attached 108 Infantry Bde Hq having taken rats. to ACHEUX returned to Head Quarters under 2/Lt Pratt.	HPH
"	7.2.16		9 wagons under Lieut Hoskins attached to 13 R.S. Ryder ages proceeding to MESNIL returned to Head Quarters	HPH
"	8.2.16		9 wagons under 2/Lieut Cheetle, no. 1 Section Attached 11 Royal Irish Rifles ages proceeding to ENGLEBELMER returned to Head Quarters	HPH
"	9.2.16		9 wagons under Lieut Hoskins proceeded to CAMAPLES for transport duty with 11th Royal Inniskilling Fusiliers on latter moving to trenches.	HPH
"	10.2.16		8 wagons under Lieut Inges. attached 12 Royal Irish Rifles ages proceeding with latter to MESNIL returned Head Quarters.	HPH

WAR DIARY or INTELLIGENCE SUMMARY

Army Form C. 2118

II Continued

Main Dressing Stn. Coxyde

(Erase heading not required.)

Place	Date	Hour	Summary of Events and Information	Remarks and references to Appendices
ST OUEN	10.2.16		9 Waggons under Lieut Hoskins attached 113th Royal Innishilling Fusiliers having accompanied the Regiment to RCHEUX returned to Head Quarters	#PH
"	"		Major W Graham R.A.M. returned from leave and assumed command of No 2 Section	#Pf

J W Crombie Lt
Lt. WSP

1875 Wt. W593/826 1,000,000 4/15 J.B.C. & A. A.D.S.S./Forms/C. 2118.

Army Form C. 2118

WAR DIARY
or
INTELLIGENCE SUMMARY
(Erase heading not required.)

Mob: 5th Army Corps
E II Corps

Instructions regarding War Diaries and Intelligence Summaries are contained in F.S. Regs., Part II. and the Staff Manual respectively. Title Pages will be prepared in manuscript.

Place	Date	Hour	Summary of Events and Information	Remarks and references to Appendices
Headquarters ST. OUEN 11.2.16			Remainder of No 3 Section proceeded to HEBUTERNE to join Section already in Position.	
"	11.2.16		Officers 1, other Ranks 80, Horses 64, Wagons 21. Field Ops went on Tomn proceeded with above to scout in enemy wagon.	#24
"	14.2.16		Hart Work & R.A. news but important Prints and notes kind of Reference.	#24
"	15.2.16		Capt G.W. Lee R.F.A. proceeded to CAYEUX for attachment to 143rd Bde R.F.A. Lt Colonel Thornton, Lieut Capt Hughes, Lieut Chisholm, Lieut Hagg uk 3nd 0 3 Orderlies proceeded to the front for instruction. Major Graham assumed Command at St Ouen —	3/2
"	18.2.16		Lt Col: Thornton and party returned to Bohain and Col: Thornton assumed Command.	#24
"	19.2.16		Lieut A.W. Julian R.F.A. assumed command of No4 Station.	#24
"	20.2.16		Captain Lee R.F.A. and Lieut M Bourne R.A.M.C. proceeded to ACHEUX and Lieut to Cheslin and Bice to VILLER BOCAGE for duty on side of Lieut Lochya.	#24
"	27.2.16		The following details proceeded to Mt. RENAULT FERME for attachment to 46th Division. 1 Runpiet (Saddler) 13 Other Ranks. 1 Horse. 20 Mules. 3 G.S. wagons. 1 M.S. B.X.	#24

Army Form C. 2118

WAR DIARY
or
☰ II Corps INTELLIGENCE SUMMARY

(Erase heading not required.)

Main Du l'Armé Col

Instructions regarding War Diaries and Intelligence Summaries are contained in F.S. Regs., Part II. and the Staff Manual respectively. Title Pages will be prepared in manuscript.

Place	Date	Hour	Summary of Events and Information	Remarks and references to Appendices
ST OUEN	22.2.16		Lieut H.J Lockyer R.F.A joined column	H.E.N
"	23.2.16		Major Brunton and 2nd Lieut S Gatkins arrived and from ST OUEN proceeded to PRENSEVILLERS, where on the march orders were received to proceed to LA VICOGNE and LE VAL de MAISON and arrive further orders. Head Quarters and MT section North up billets at LA VICOGNE 10th W.T Division billeted at LE VAL de MAISON. Heavy rain was experienced during the march.	H.E.N
"	24.2.16		Lieut W.P Fitzgerald struck off strength on posting to 11th Special Works Battery Army 14th Corps M?of A dated 19th Feby 1916.	H.E.N
LA VICOGNE	25.2.16		Lieut S.W Davies R.F.A and Lieut J.A Price R.F.A attached on posting to division from Home.	H.E.N

Whow impostume
Lt 25? {water} Div

1875 Wt. W593/826 1,000,000 4/15 J.B.C. & A. A.D.S.S./Forms/C. 2118.

86 DWA C

VOT 35

36

173rd Bde: R.A.
Vol: 4

36th D.A.C.
Vol: IV

WAR DIARY or INTELLIGENCE SUMMARY

Army Form C. 2118

Unit: Divl Ammn Col

Place	Date	Hour	Summary of Events and Information	Remarks and references to Appendices
LAVICOGNE	1-3-16		Column Head Quarters and No.1 Section moved from LA VICOGNE via BEAUQUESNE, RAINCHEVAL to ARQUEVES taking up billets in later place.	JCH
ARQUEVES	3.3.16		All Ammunition in charge of Column was handed over to H.S. Divl. Ammn Col. No. 344.59. S.Q.M.S. Walters returned to Depôt and No. 53039. Sergt J Wheeler returned to ranks for inefficiency Authy W Scott No.V/144.19 dt 29-2-16. under Sec 185 Army Act.	JCH
"	"		No.98063 Corpl. Durrant promoted Sergeant vice Wheeler reduced.	JCH
BELLE EGLISE	"		No.3 Section at BELLE EGLISE rejoined unit for duty having completed railway work, but remains in detachment at BELLE EGLISE.	JCH
ARQUEVES	4-3-16		Lieut J.A. Price R.F.A. no posted as Lieutenant and 2nd Lieut E.W. Deurie R.F.A. is posted to 154th Bde R.F.A.	JCH
"	5-3-16		No.2 Section rejoins Column from VAL de MAISON at ARQUEVES and takes up billets at latter place.	
"	"	9 a.m.	The Column takes over from H.S. Divl Ammn. Col. and commences supply of Ammunition to the Divisions in action, with refilling point at FORCEVILLE under command of Lieut R.F. Pritchard R.F.A. No.3 Section at BELLE EGLISE and Head Qrs under No.3.1 and 2 Sections at ARQUEVES. No.39043. B.Q.M.S. I.J. Barry goes to duty from 142 Bde R.F.A.	JCH

Army Form C. 2118

WAR DIARY
or
INTELLIGENCE SUMMARY

(Erase heading not required.)

36th D/S Ammn Col

Instructions regarding War Diaries and Intelligence Summaries are contained in F. S. Regs., Part II. and the Staff Manual respectively. Title Pages will be prepared in manuscript.

Place	Date	Hour	Summary of Events and Information	Remarks and references to Appendices
ARQUEVES	17.3.16		2Lieut W. Humphrey R.F.A. joined for duty from 143rd Bde R.F.A.	
"	18.3.16		2Lieut E.R. Price Davies to 153rd Bde R.F.A. and struck off strength	
"	19.3.16		2Lieut E. Browne joined for duty from Base	
	23.3.16		Lieut P.J. Gignoux joined for duty from 153 Brigade R.F.A.	
	28.3.16		2Lieut J.E. Hicks Wilson joined for duty from Base.	
"	"		2Lieut Gwynne Norton Do	
	31.3.16		The Column moved from ARQUEVES via RANCHEVAL to PUCHEVILLERS taking up billets in latter place.	
	31.4.16		2Lieut G. Breese Bowen joined for duty from Base.	
	31.4.16		2Lieut J. Clayton Hardie joined for duty from Base.	

J.M. Mordaunt Lt Col
Commanding
36th Divl. Ammn Column.

Army Form C. 2118

6
Vol 4

WAR DIARY

INTELLIGENCE SUMMARY

36th D. Div¹ Amn. Col.

(Erase heading not required.)

Place	Date	Hour	Summary of Events and Information	Remarks and references to Appendices
PUCHEVILLERS	9.4.16	32	Lieut. H.F. Lockyer RFA. having been posted to the 164th Bde. RFA. is struck off the strength	HEH
...	16.4.16		Capt. W.H. Pawson RFA. having joined from home is taken on the strength	HEH
...	25.4.16		Lieut. J.W. Browne having been posted to 173rd Bde RFA. is struck off the strength	HEH
...	28.4.16		Col. S.Y. Thornton RFA. having proceeded on leave Capt. J.R. Hobson RFA assumes command of column.	HEH

Field
1-5-16

John R Hobson Capt. RFA
Commanding 36th D Div¹ Amn. Col.

WAR DIARY or INTELLIGENCE SUMMARY

Army Form C. 2118

36 D Div Amm. Col. Vol 5

Place	Date MAY	Hour	Summary of Events and Information	Remarks and references to Appendices
Puchevillers	3.6.16		Lieut L. Horton R.F.A. posted to T. 36. T.M. Battery and struck off strength	H.E.A
"	"		No 30876. Driver W. Bell slightly wounded whilst on fatigue at MARTINSART	H.E.A
"	4.6.16		1st Btl. W. Thornton R.F.A. rejoined from leave and assumed command of column	H.E.A
"	8.6.16		Lieut J. Clayton started R.F.A. posted to 153 Bde R.F.A. and struck off strength	H.E.A
"	16.6.16		Commencement of Re-organization of column to 4 sections and taking the place of Brigade Amm. Columns. 153rd B.A.C. forms (No 1 Section) B Echelon being brought up to strength by details from 154, 142, & 173 B.A.C.'s under command of Capt W.H. Lee R.F.A.	H.E.A
"	14.6.16		Additional personnel and horses to bring A Echelon up to strength received from B.A.C.'s	H.E.A
"	18.6.16		Wagons and equipment received from B.A.C.'s and 2/5 wagons to complete A Echelon formed	H.E.A
"	20.6.16		Head quarters and No2 Section move from Puchevillers to Hedauville and take over supply of ammunition to Batteries. No 1 and 2 Sections move from Puchevillers to Varennes. D. Echelon move from Hedauville to Harponville	H.E.A

Lieut J. Clayton Hardie R.F.A. Reinforcmt ? Section R.F.A. and Lieut L. Catchin R.F.A. posted to B Section. Lieut W.K. Purdie posted from 142/3 R.F.A. to No 2 Section

1875 Wt. W593/826 1,000,000 4/15 J.B.C. & A. A.D.S.S./Forms/C. 2118.

Army Form C. 2118

WAR DIARY
or
INTELLIGENCE SUMMARY

36 P Divⁿ Ammn Col

(Erase heading not required.)

Place	Date	Hour	Summary of Events and Information	Remarks and references to Appendices
HÉDAUVILLE	28.6.16		Capt H.E. Putt R.F.A. posted from 142ᵈ Bde. R.F.A. and assumes command of No 2. Section.	HEA
	1ˢᵗ June 1916			

Wharton
Lt.Col. R. F. A.
Cmdg. 36th (West Ham) Divl. Ammunition Column

Army Form C. 2118

WAR DIARY
of
INTELLIGENCE SUMMARY
(Erase heading not required.)

36th Divn Ammn Col
Vol 6

Instructions regarding War Diaries and Intelligence Summaries are contained in F.S. Regs., Part II. and the Staff Manual respectively. Title Pages will be prepared in manuscript.

Place	Date	Hour	Summary of Events and Information	Remarks and references to Appendices
Hedauville	7.6.16		Lieut J Breeze Bonn. posted to 143 Bde R.F.A. is struck off strength of Column	HQN
"	"		" J Pursey " " 142 Bde R.F.A. " " " " "	HQN
"	8.6.16		Column employed in supply ammunition to Batteries for dumps	HQN
"	9.6.16		— ditto —	HQN
"	10.6.16		ditto	HQN
"	11.6.16		ditto	HQN
"	12.6.16		ditto	HQN
"	13.6.16		ditto	HQN
"	14.6.16		Time advanced one hour at 11 pm to coincide with time adopted by French Government	HQN
"	"		Supply of Ammunition continued	HQN
"	15.6.16		ditto	HQN
"	16.6.16		ditto	HQN
"	17.6.16		Lieut AW Julian posted to 153rd Bde R.F.A.	HQN
"	"		" R Hunton posted from 4 Trench Mortar Battery is taken on strength	HQN
"	"		Supply of Ammunition continued	HQN
"	18.6.16		ditto	HQN
"	19.6.16		Lieut P.J. Flanagan posted to 173 Bde R.F.A. is struck off strength	HQN
"	"		Lieut J Breeze Bonn " " from 173 " " " " is taken on the strength	HQN
"	"		Ammunition Supply continued	HQN
"	20.6.16		ditto	HQN
"	21.6.16		ditto	HQN
"	22.6.16		ditto	HQN

WAR DIARY
or
INTELLIGENCE SUMMARY

(Erase heading not required.)

Army Form C. 2118

36 D.D. in Ammn Col.

Place	Date	Hour	Summary of Events and Information	Remarks and references to Appendices
Neuville	22.6.16		Lieut H. J. Lothing posted to M3 Bde R.F.A. no struck off the strength	H.E.A
"	—		No 2 Section under the command of Capt H.E. Pitt moved from Head Quarters to Neuville and increased Ammunition Supply continued ditto ditto	H.E.A H.E.A H.E.A
"	24.6.16			
"	—			
"	25.6.16		Head Quarters of Column move to Hedauville Wood and prepare reserve dump of Ammunition	H.E.A
"	26.6.16		Lieut L. J. Strahan Bomr Gunner Gunner Swain Fogarty Sell Shepherd Potter Hone Walker Roses Ford congratulations by G.O.C. Re 2.6.5 Bish. Div. Arty for the way in which they conveyed ammunition to Harvel under fire	H.E.A
"	30.6.16		Lieut G.O. Dyer posted to 175 Bde. R.F.A. no struck off the strength Ammunition supply direct onwards side from Dumps ditto	H.E.A H.E.A H.E.A
			1 – 4 – 6	

H.C. Hughes Lieut Adj R.F.A.

J.M.Col. R.F.A.

WAR DIARY or INTELLIGENCE SUMMARY

Army Form C. 2118

36 July
36 D^n Amm^n Col

Place	Date	Hour	Summary of Events and Information	Remarks and references to Appendices
Hédauville	1-7-16		Ammunition supplied direct to wagon lines	HCM
"	2-7-16		Supply of Ammunition was handed over at 8 p.m. to 49th D.A.C.	HCM
"	3-7-16		Head Quarters & Echelons and loading table moved from Hédauville Wood to Varennes.	HCM
Varennes	5-7-16		A Convoy returning with empty ammunition wagons through Hédauville was shelled and the following men wounded. Lt Col^m B^ty Strutt, Halsted, Lewis & Smith and drivers and advanced workshops.	HCM
			No 2 Section under command of Capt J. E. Pike and a proportion of B Echelon under 2 Lieut J. Clayton Hardie proceeded to Millencourt and Henencourt Wood to gun 125 R.F.A. for artillery of ammunition	HCM HCM
"	6-7-16		Batteries of 36 D Division attached to 23 Division. Capt Strutt R.F.A. admitted to Hospital. Field 2/Lt Ibrahim and Lieut J.J. Phelan taken to 142 B^de R.F.A. the attack... off the attempts	HCM HCM
"	9-7-16		Lieut E. A. Benford taken from 153 B^de R.F.A. was taken in attempt and taken to B. Echelon	HCM
"	10-7-16		"B" Echelon consisting of wet wagons of 3 A.A. and Grenade moved by road from Hédauville to Beauval under command of Capt Lowrie R.F.A.	HCM
	11-7-16		2 Lieut A.D. Thurston India Home and struck off strength	HCM

WAR DIARY or INTELLIGENCE SUMMARY

Army Form C. 2118

36 D Div¹ "Amm" Col

VII

Place	Date	Hour	Summary of Events and Information	Remarks and references to Appendices
Varennes	12.7.16		No 2 Section under Capt. H.P. Gee and detachment of "B" Echelon rejoined Column after attachment to 12th D.A.C.	HPG
"	13.7.16		Preparation for move to 2nd Army Area	HPG
"	14.7.16		The Column marched by road to AUTHIEULE and bivouaced	HPG
On line of march	15.7.16		" " " " VACQUERIE DE BOURG "	HPG
"	16.7.16		" " " " WAVRANS "	HPG
"	14.7.16		" " " " DÉLETTE "	HPG
"	18.7.16		" " " " TOURNEHEM " and S.A.A. Section	HPG
TOURNEHEM	19.7.16		at GUEMY. The Column halted	HPG
"	20.7.16		About 8 Horses R.A. admitted to Hospital	HPG
"	21.7.16		The Column marched by road to RENESCURES and bivouaced less SAA	HPG
Line of march	24.7.16		Section which marched to NORDAUSQUES. The Column marched by road to MIDDENAKVER and bivouaced	HPG
"	22.7.16		The Column marched by road to positions East of BAILLEUL and delivered the	HPG
"			2nd D.A.C. Their war ammunition supply and Rent Section	HPG

Army Form C. 2118

WAR DIARY
or
INTELLIGENCE SUMMARY
(Erase heading not required.)

Place	Date	Hour	Summary of Events and Information	Remarks and references to Appendices
E of BAILLEUL	24.7.16		No events to report	
	25.7.16		About 10 electric R.E.A admitted to hospital	
	26.7.16		About R.S. Reeceford R.E.A. added to 33rd Divisional Artillery. I.A.A Section reported behaviour. Sections and 15 Echelon reorganised as troop estimated behaviour. About 15 privates Rinker R.E.A admitted to hospital.	
	27.7.16		No events to report	
	28.7.16		ditto	
	29.7.16		ditto	
	30.7.16		ditto	
	31.7.16		ditto	

VOL 8

Army Form C. 2118.

36 Div. Ammunition Col.

WAR DIARY
or
INTELLIGENCE SUMMARY
(Erase heading not required.)

VIII

Place	Date	Hour	Summary of Events and Information	Remarks and references to Appendices
E of PARNEUL	5.8.16		Lieut B Eberle invalided to England & struck off the strength of Column	HQU
"	6.8.16		5 Privates Sick	HQU
"	15.8.16		70. was temporarily posted from X.T.M. Battery in taken into Lieut H.A. Howes joined from Base	HQU
"	19.8.16		Corp H.C. Pratt promoted to 1st Cl. Corp. R.A.M. is attached up etc.	HQU
"			Lieut A Rushy " from 19.3.16 - to taken on the strength and armed runrank of No. 2 Section	HQU
"	23.8.16		Lieut H.A. Howes posted to 41st Brigade Ammunition Coly; is struck off the strength of column	HQU
"	14.8.16 to 31.8.16		The Column was employed in bringing lines for the units served	HQU

[signature]

10th Div. A.C.

Army Form C. 2118

WAR DIARY
or
INTELLIGENCE SUMMARY

(Erase heading not required.)

Instructions regarding War Diaries and Intelligence Summaries are contained in F. S. Regs., Part II. and the Staff Manual respectively. Title Pages will be prepared in manuscript.

IX 3rd Div: Ammn. Col.

Place	Date	Hour	Summary of Events and Information	Remarks and references to Appendices
E. of BAILLEUL	19.9.15		Artillery Brigades being reorganised. Butters horses and Gun were handed over to O. Eshelon.	A.21
			The Column now employed in building horse standings etc	A.24

Wihornton
Lt. Col. R.F.A.
Com'dg 30th (West Ham) Div. Ammunition Column

1875 Wt. W593/826 1,000,000 4/15 J.B.C. & A. A.D.S.S./Forms/C. 2118.

Army Form C. 2118

Vol 10

WAR DIARY
or
INTELLIGENCE SUMMARY
(Erase heading not required.)

36th Div" Amm" Col

Place	Date	Hour	Summary of Events and Information	Remarks and references to Appendices
E. of BAINEUX	6.10.16		"A" Echelon exchanged with "B" Echelon their trucks for horses	A.F.94
			The Column continued in drawing Winter Clothing etc	A.F.94

Wilton
Lt. Col. R.F.A.
Comdg 36th (West Ham) Divl Ammunition Column

WAR DIARY
or
INTELLIGENCE SUMMARY

Army Form C. 2118

36 Div: Amm Col

Place	Date	Hour	Summary of Events and Information	Remarks and references to Appendices
Palmeston	1914		Artillery Brigades being reorganised. Surplus Horses and Stores been handed over to "B" Echelon.	AR1
			The column now employed in collecting horse clothing etc	AR2

Thornton
Bt. Col. R.F.A.
Comdg. 36th (West Ham) Divl. Ammunition Column

Army Form C. 2118

WAR DIARY
or
INTELLIGENCE SUMMARY
(Erase heading not required.)

8 D.A.C. R.F.A.

Vol XI

80th DIVISIONAL AMMUNITION COLUMN.
No. D.Y.02.36
Date 4.12.16

Place	Date	Hour	Summary of Events and Information	Remarks and references to Appendices
E. of Bainzen	Nov. 1916		Column worked in completing Standings for horses and Accommodation for men.	AEH

Signed
Lt Col. R.F.A.
Comdg 38th (Welsh) Ham Divl Ammunition Column

WAR DIARY

Army Form C. 2118

Intelligence Summary 36th D.A.C. Vol 12

Place	Date	Hour	Summary of Events and Information	Remarks and references to Appendices
E. of BAILLEUL	23.12.16		Lieut H.K. Purdy joined 16 1/72nd Bde R.F.A. and is struck off the strength of Column.	3/31
	24.12.16		Lieut J Stilwell and Lieut A Reid posted on granted Commissions from the ranks, from HQ Division	5/31
	26.12.16		Lieut A. Wright posted to 1/72" Bde R.F.A. and Lieut L.J. Preston joined 1/83rd Bde R.F.A. and are struck off the strength	9/31
	31.12.16		The Column was employed during the month in assisting in ascertaining for horses and accommodation for men.	1/31

31-1-'16

Signature

Comdg. 36th (East Ham) Divl. Ammunition Column
Bt. Col. R.F.A.

Army Form C. 2118

WAR DIARY
~~INTELLIGENCE SUMMARY~~
(Erase heading not required.)

36 D A C

Vol 13

Instructions regarding War Diaries and Intelligence Summaries are contained in F.S. Regs, Part II. and the Staff Manual respectively. Title Pages will be prepared in manuscript.

XIII

Place	Date	Hour	Summary of Events and Information	Remarks and references to Appendices
E.J.	4-1-19		Mentioned in Despatches. London Gazette dated. 1-1-19.	
BAILLEUL	1-1-19 to 31-1-19		Lt. Col. (Bt: Col.) B.V. Thornton. R.A. Lieut & adjt. H.Q. Hughes R.F.A. Lieut. L.J. Hoskins R.F.A. The Column was employed in constructing Horse Standings and accommodation for men	HQH HQH
	31/1/19			

N. Graham
Major R.F.A.
Comdg 36th (West Ham) Div. Ammunition Column

Army Form C. 2118

WAR DIARY
or
INTELLIGENCE SUMMARY
(Erase heading not required.)

Instructions regarding War Diaries and Intelligence Summaries are contained in F. S. Regs., Part II. and the Staff Manual respectively. Title Pages will be prepared in manuscript.

Place	Date	Hour	Summary of Events and Information	Remarks and references to Appendices
In the Field nr BAILLEUL	14.2.17		Reorganization carried out. No 1 Section disbanded.	AWR
"	15.2.17		Lt Col — S.V. Thornton R.F.A Comdg 36" D.A.C is struck off the strength of the 36" Division with effect from 15" February 1917 Auth: Second Army A/1727 dated 15" February 1917	AWR
"	23.2.17		Lieut + Adjt W.A. Edmiston joined for duty from 172 Bde R.F.A (disbanded 22.2.17) vice Lieut H.E. Hughes.	AWR
"	25.2.17		Capt. J. H.G. Riley R.H.A. assumed Command of the Column with effect from 25.2.17.	AWR

A.W. Riley
Lt. Col. R.F.A.
Commanding 36th D.A.C.

Army Form C. 2118

WAR DIARY
or
INTELLIGENCE SUMMARY
(Erase heading not required.)

Vol. 15

Place	Date	Hour	Summary of Events and Information	Remarks and references to Appendices
N.E. of BAILLEUL	28-3-17		Lieut. C. WILLIAMSON, R.F.A. Commanding No 2 Section, 36th D.A.C. is posted to 153rd Bde. R.F.A. with effect from 28-3-17.	A/R
			Captain W. H. PAWSON, R.F.A. posted to 36th D.A.C. to Command No 2 Section with effect from 28-3-17.	
	31.3.17.		W. Riley
Lieut. Col. R.F.A.
Commanding 36th D.A.C.	

Army Form C. 2118

WAR DIARY
or
INTELLIGENCE SUMMARY
(Erase heading not required.)

36th Div. Ammn. Col. July 16

Place	Date	Hour	Summary of Events and Information	Remarks and references to Appendices
N.E. of BAILLEUL	14/7		2/Lieut. H.S.E. Hunt, R.F.A. struck off the strength with effect from 12/7/7. Authority 2nd Army R.A. 9/73 of 12/7/7. 2/Lieut. G. Sorray R.F.A. is brought on the strength with effect from 14/7/17.	A/R A/R
	26		2/Lieut A.A. Ward R.F.A. is brought on the strength with effect from 26/7/17. 2/Lieut. E.W.J. Edwardes posted to 173rd Bde R.F.A. with effect from 26/7/17.	A/R A/R

A.W.Riley Lieut Col. R.F.A.
Commanding 36th D.A.C.

Army Form C. 2118

WAR DIARY
or
INTELLIGENCE SUMMARY

36th Div. Ammunition Column

(Erase heading not required.)

Vol 17

Place	Date	Hour	Summary of Events and Information	Remarks and references to Appendices
N.E. of BAILLEUL	1/5/17	–	Lieut. M.J. BEAVIS. R.F.A. taken on strength from this date.	
	12/5/17	–	Commenced taking over and receiving large quantities of Ammunition.	
	14/5/17	–	2nd Lieut. L.T. HASKINS. R.F.A. Posted from Z 36th T.M. Bty to No 2 Section with effect from this date.	
	–	–	2nd Lieut. F.W.H. MAGEE and 2nd Lieut. F.I. COTCHING to be temp. Lieuts. London Gazette dated 12-5-1917.	
	16/5/17	–	2nd Lieut. N.S. BARRY. R.F.A. taken on strength from this date.	
	18/5/17	–	2nd Lieut. E. WIGHT. R.F.A. taken on strength from this date and attached to 173rd Bde R.F.A.	
	20/5/17	–	2nd Lieut. A.A. WARD. R.F.A. attached to X 36th T.M. Bty with effect from this date.	
	–	–	2nd Lieut. H.H. MORRIS. R.F.A. Posted to 173rd Bde. R.F.A. with effect from 19-5-1917.	
	24/5/17	–	2nd Lieut. R.N. STRANGER. R.F.A. Posted to V.36th T.M. Bty with effect from 24-5-1917.	
	–	–	Lieut. M.J. BEAVIS. R.F.A. struck off the strength with effect from 23-5-1917.	
	27/5/17	–	Enemy shelled this area during the night 27-28th May 1917. No Casualties in this Unit.	
	28/5/17	–	Enemy again shelled this area wounding one man and killing one horse.	
	29/5/17	–	Owing to enemy shell fire horses of H.Q., No 1 and 2 Sections were moved at night to a field further west.	

WAR DIARY
INTELLIGENCE SUMMARY

Army Form C. 2118

Place	Date	Hour	Summary of Events and Information	Remarks and references to Appendices
N.E. of BAILLEUL.	30/5/17	—	Horses again moved at night to field west of Cte de Poperinghe. Enemy again shelled Wagon Line area. Two men and eight mules wounded while out with convoy.	A.R. A.R.
	3/5/17	—	Horses moved to field west of Cte de Poperinghe during night.	

1/6/17.

A.R. Riley Lieut. Colonel. R.F.A.
Commanding, 36th Divisional Ammunition Column.

Army Form C. 2118

WAR DIARY
or
INTELLIGENCE SUMMARY
(Erase heading not required.)

Place	Date	Hour	Summary of Events and Information	Remarks and references to Appendices
N.E. of BAILLEUL	1/5/17	-	Lieut. M.J. BEAVIS. R.F.A. taken on strength from this date.	
	12/5/17	-	Commenced taking over and receiving large quantities of Ammunition.	
	14/5/17	-	2nd Lieut. L.J. HASKINS. R.F.A. Posted from Z 36th T.M. Bty to No 2 Section with effect from this date.	
	-	-	2nd Lieuts. F.W.H. MAGEE and 2nd Lieut. F.I. COTCHING to be temp. Lieuts. London Gazette dated 12-5-1917.	
	16/5/17	-	2nd Lieut. N.S. BARRY. R.F.A. taken on strength from this date.	
	18/5/17	-	Lieut. E. WIGHT. R.F.A. taken on strength from this date and attached to 173rd Bde R.F.A.	
	20/5/17	-	2nd Lieut. A.A. WARD. R.F.A. attached to X 36 T.M. Bty with effect from this date.	
	-	-	2nd Lieut. H.H. MORRIS. R.F.A. Posted to 173rd Bde. R.F.A. with effect from 19-5-1917.	
	24/5/17	-	2nd Lieut. R.N. STRANGER. R.F.A. Posted to V 36th T.M. Bty with effect from 25-5-1917.	
	-	-	Lieut. M.J. BEAVIS. R.F.A. struck off the strength with effect from 27th-28th May 1917. No casualties in this Unit.	
	27/5/17	-	Enemy shelled this area during the night 27th-28th May 1917. No casualties in this Unit.	
	28/5/17	-	Enemy again shelled this area wounding one man and killing one horse.	
	29/5/17	-	Owing to enemy shell fire horses of M.O's No 1 and 2 Sections were moved at night to a field further west.	

Army Form C. 2118

WAR DIARY
or
INTELLIGENCE SUMMARY
(Erase heading not required.)

Place	Date	Hour	Summary of Events and Information	Remarks and references to Appendices
N.E. of BAILLEUL	30/7	—	Horses again moved at night to field west of C^t de Yperinghe. Enemy again shelled Wagon Line area. Two men and eight mules wounded while out with convoy.	RWS RWR
	31/7	—	Horses moved to field west of C^t de Yperinghe during night.	
	1/8/17			

A.H. Riley Lieut. Colonel. R.F.A.
Commanding, 36th Divisional Ammunition Column

Army Form C. 2118

WAR DIARY
or
INTELLIGENCE SUMMARY

36th Divn Ammunition Column   Vol 18

(Erase heading not required.)

Instructions regarding War Diaries and Intelligence Summaries are contained in F.S. Regs., Part II. and the Staff Manual respectively. Title Pages will be prepared in manuscript.

Place	Date	Hour	Summary of Events and Information	Remarks and references to Appendices
N.E. BAILLEUL	1/7/17		Enemy shelled this area on the night of the 1/7. No casualties in this Unit.	AAR
	2/7/17		Enemy Aeroplane dropped bombs in this area on the night of the 1/7. No casualties in this Unit	AAR
	3/7/17		Enemy shelled this area on the night of the 2/7. No casualties in this Unit	AAR
	–		do 3/7/17 do	AAR
	4/7/17		Stampede of Horses in one section. 4 men injured.	AAR
	5/7/17		Enemy shelled this area on the night of the 4/7. No casualties in this Unit	AAR
	6/7/17		do 5/7/17 do	AAR
	7/7/17		do 6/7/17 do	AAR
	–		do 7/7/17 do	AAR
	8/7/17		Usual Routine – Supply of Ammunition.	AAR
	9/7/17		do	AAR
	10/7/17		do	AAR

Army Form C. 2118

WAR DIARY or INTELLIGENCE SUMMARY

(Erase heading not required.)

Place	Date	Hour	Summary of Events and Information	Remarks and references to Appendices
N.E. BAILLEUL.	17/7/17	—	Lieut. W.A. EDMENSON. R.F.A. (S.R.) relinquishes the Appointment of Adjutant, 36th Divisional Ammunition Column with effect from 16/7/17.	A.W.R.
	—	—	Lieut. F.W.H. MAGEE. R.F.A. Assumes the duties of Adjutant, 36th Divisional Ammunition Column with effect from 16/7/17.	A.W.R.
	—	—	Lieut. W.A. EDMENSON. R.F.A. Posted as Second in Command to D/173 Bde R.F.A. with effect from 17/7/17.	A.W.R.
	18/7/17	—	Captain. G.W. LEE. R.F.A. Posted as Second in Command to B/173 Bde R.F.A. with effect from 17/7/17.	A.W.R.
	—	—	Lieut. C. WILLIAMSON. R.F.A. Joined from 153 Bde R.F.A. to Command 'B' Echelon, 36th Divisional Ammunition Column, with effect from 17/7/17.	A.W.R.
	21/7/17	—	2nd Lieut. R.E.N. BRADEN. R.F.A. Taken on the strength with effect from 17/7/17.	A.W.R.
	24/7/17	—	Headquarters and 'A' Echelon moved from N.E. BAILLEUL to W. of BAILLEUL on the 21/7/17.	A.W.R.
	—	—	Headquarters, 'A' and 'B' Echelon moved from W. of BAILLEUL to DRANOUTRE on the 24/7/17.	A.W.R.
	—	—	2nd Lieut. F.R. LEBISH. R.F.A. Taken on strength from this date.	A.W.R.
	25/7/17	—	2nd Lieut. T.J. LACEY. R.F.A. Taken on strength from this date.	A.W.R.
	—	—	Lieut. J.F. KENNEDY. R.F.A. Joined from D/173 Bde R.F.A. to Command No 2 Section with effect from 25/7/17.	A.W.R.
	—	—	Captain. W.H. PAWSON. R.F.A. of England on the 25/7/17 struck off the strength of the 36th D.A.C.	A.W.R.

Army Form C. 2118

WAR DIARY
or
INTELLIGENCE SUMMARY
(Erase heading not required.)

Instructions regarding War Diaries and Intelligence Summaries are contained in F. S. Regs., Part II. and the Staff Manual respectively. Title Pages will be prepared in manuscript.

Place	Date	Hour	Summary of Events and Information	Remarks and references to Appendices
DRANOUTRE.	26/7		2/Lieut. F. R. LEBISH. RFA. Posted to D/173 Bde RFA. with effect from 26/7.	
	27/7		Lieut. G. J. ATKINS. RFA. Taken on the strength with effect from 27/7.	
			2/Lieut. T. J. LACEY. RFA. Posted to 173 Bde RFA with effect from 27/7.	

1/7/7.

A. O'Riley Lieut. Col. R.F.A.
Commanding, 36th Divisional Ammunition Column.

Army Form C. 2118

WAR DIARY
or
INTELLIGENCE SUMMARY

(Erase heading not required.)

36th D.A.C.

Vol 19

Instructions regarding War Diaries and Intelligence Summaries are contained in F.S. Regs., Part II. and the Staff Manual respectively. Title Pages will be prepared in manuscript.

Place	Date	Hour	Summary of Events and Information	Remarks and references to Appendices
DRANOUTRE	2/7/17		2nd Lieut. W.R. PICKETT. R.F.A. Joined from R.H. & R.F.A. Base 2-7-17. Posted to No.1 Section.	A/M/R
	"		" J.R. WRIGHT. R.F.A. — do —	A/M/R
	"		" E.M.P. FISHER. R.F.A. — do — 2 "B" Echelon	A/M/R
	5/7/17		" L.J. HASKINS. R.F.A. Struck off the strength with effect from 1-7-17.	A/M/R
	7/7/17		" M.J.B. PITT. R.F.A. Admitted to Hospital 5/7/17.	A/M/R
	8/7/17		Headquarters "A" & "B" Echelons moved to East of Sheringhe.	A/M/R
W. of POPERINGHE	9/7/17		" " " West of Sheringhe (Water).	A/M/R
	"		Lieut. E. WIGHT R.F.A. Posted to 173rd Brigade R.F.A. on the 9/7/17.	A/M/R
	"		2nd Lieut. N.S. BARRY R.F.A. " do " to 153rd	A/M/R
	13/7/17		Lieut. F.I. COTCHING R.F.A. " " to 153rd	A/M/R
	"		2nd Lieut. A. SIMMONS R.F.A. Joined from R.H.& R.F.A. Base 13-7-17. Posted to "B" Echelon. 13/7/17	A/M/R
	15/7/17		" J.R. WRIGHT R.F.A. Posted to 173rd Brigade R.F.A. 15/7/17	A/M/R
	"		" J.W. NAYLOR R.F.A. Joined from — do —	A/M/R
	19/7/17		" A.A. WARD R.F.A. Transferred to Royal Flying Corps 19/7/17.	A/M/R
	20/7/17		Lieut. G.J. ATKINS R.F.A. Admitted to Hospital 20/7/17.	A/M/R
	23/7/17		" C. WILLIAMSON R.F.A. } Authority given by Divisional Commander	A/M/R
			" J.F. KENNEDY R.F.A. } to wear the badges of Captain.	A/M/R
	25/7/17		2nd Lieut. R.E.N. BRADEN R.F.A. Posted to 173rd Brigade R.F.A. 25/7/17.	A/M/R

1875 Wt. W593/826 1,000,000 4/15 J.B.C. & A. A.D.S.S./Forms/C. 2118.

WAR DIARY
or
INTELLIGENCE SUMMARY
(Erase heading not required.)

Army Form C. 2118

Place	Date	Hour	Summary of Events and Information	Remarks and references to Appendices
W of Poperinghe	July 24		H.Q.r. 'A' & 'B' Echelons moved to East of Poperinghe.	AMR
E — do —	25		2nd Lieut. C.W. DYER. R.F.A. Posted to 173rd Brigade R.F.A. 25/7/17	AMR
	26		F.C. JARVIS. R.B.A. joined from RFA RGA Base 28/7/17	AMR
	27		Rev. D. KELLY. C.F.	AMR
	29		— do — " 27/7/17	AMR
	30		Rev. J.G. HARVEY. C.F. Joined Jo. O.t.6.C. H.Q. 19th Corps 29/7/17	AMR
			Lieut. (Acting Captain) J.F. KENNEDY. R.F.A. Attached as Second in Command of D/173 Bde RFA 30/7/17	AMR
			2nd Lieut. E.N. KENNEDY R.F.A. Attached from D/153rd Bde to Command No 2 Section 30/7/17	AMR
	31st		Headquarters 'A' & 'B' Echelons moved to East of VLAMERTINGHE.	AMR
	17/7 to 31/7/17		Usual Routine — Supply of Ammunition.	AMR
	17/7 to 31/7/17		Casualties caused by Enemy Shell fire :—	AMR

	OFFICERS.	O. RANKS.	ANIMALS
	NIL.	4. Killed. 15 Wounded.	15 L.D. Killed 7 L.D Wounded

1/8/17

A.M. Riley
Lt Col. R.F.A
Commanding, 36th Divisional Ammunition Column

WAR DIARY
or
INTELLIGENCE SUMMARY

36" D.A. Column

Army Form C. 2118

Vol 20

Place	Date	Hour	Summary of Events and Information	Remarks and references to Appendices
EAST of VLAMEN-TINGHE	15/9/17		Capt. R.F.T. COLSELL. RFA. Joined from Base photo to No 2 Section	
			Lieut. D.J. WHEATLEY. RFA — do — 1	
			2nd Lieut. C.J.A. PENNECK. RFA — do — 3 9/17	
	16/9/17		J. LAMB RFA. "Killed in Action" on the 16 9/17.	
	17/9/17		Nouse Routine — Supply of Ammunition	
	18/9/17		Enemy Bombs fell in Camp Area	
	19/9/17		Nouse Routine — Supply of Ammunition.	
	20/9/17		Enemy Bomb fell in Camp area.	
			2nd Lieut. G. ISMAY. RFA. Posted from No 1 to No 2 Section.	
	21/9/17		Nouse Routine — Supply of Ammunition.	
	22/9/17		Handed over the supply of Ammunition to 55th D.A.C.	
			2nd Lieut. D.A. SMITH. RFA. Posted from Base to No 2 Section	
			(2nd Lieut) C. WILLIAMSON. RFA. to be Acting Captain whilst in command	
			of B Echelon with effect from 17-6-17.	
	23/9/17		Marched through Poperinghe to Manescelle Area.	
			2nd Lieut. F.C. JARVIS. RFA Posted from No 2 to No 1 Section	
	24/9/17		Usual Routine	
	25/9/17			
	26/9/17		Lieut. J.W. NAYLOR. RFA. Proceeds to England. Struck off Strength.	
	27/9/17		Inspection by R.G.R.A. who spoke appreciative of work done during recent operations.	
	28/9/17		Usual routine	
	29/9/17		Marched to Caoul and entrained for BAPAUME en route for IV Corps Area.	

WAR DIARY
INTELLIGENCE SUMMARY

Army Form C. 2118

Place	Date	Hour	Summary of Events and Information	Remarks and references to Appendices
LE MESNIL	30/8/17		Arrival at Bapaume & marches through Rocquigny to temporary camp near LE MESNIL.	AWR
	14/7		T. Lieut. F.W.H. MAGEE R.F.A.	AWR
	18/8/17		Authy. to wear Badges of Captain whilst performing the duties of Adjutant.	AWR
	31/8/17		Casualties caused by Enemy Shells & Bombs during march.	AWR
			Officer. Killed. 1. Wounded. Nil.	
			Other Ranks. Killed. 2. Wounded. 4.	
			Animals. Killed. 53. Wounded. 45.	

Comdg. 36th Divisional Ammunition Column

WAR DIARY
or
INTELLIGENCE SUMMARY 36th Div. Ammunition Column

(Erase heading not required.)

Army Form C. 2118

Instructions regarding War Diaries and Intelligence Summaries are contained in F. S. Regs., Part II. and the Staff Manual respectively. Title Pages will be prepared in manuscript.

WO 21

Place	Date	Hour	Summary of Events and Information	Remarks and references to Appendices
Le Mesnil	1st		Usual Routine – Supply of Ammunition.	AAR
	2nd		do also Amn Refilling Point & Bomb Store	AAR
	3rd		B.H.Q. marches from Le Mesnil to Equancourt and took over camp vacated by 9th D.A.C.	AAR
Equancourt	4th		Building of Winter Standings begun.	AAR
			Usual Routine – Supply of Ammunition.	AAR
	5th		do	AAR
	6th		Section training begun.	AAR
			No 2 Section from 6.9.17 to 15.9.17	AAR
	7th		Usual Routine – Supply of Ammunition.	AAR
	8th		2nd Lieut. H. Iddon R.F.A. Posted from No 2 to No 1 Section	AAR
	9th		Usual Routine – Supply of Ammunition	AAR
	10th		do	AAR
			do	AAR
	11th		Re-organization of D.A.C. completed.	AAR
			Usual Routine Supply of Ammunition	AAR
	12th		do	AAR
	13th		do	AAR
	14th		do	AAR
	15th		No 2 Section complete period of training	AAR

Army Form C. 2118

WAR DIARY
or
INTELLIGENCE SUMMARY
(Erase heading not required.)

Instructions regarding War Diaries and Intelligence Summaries are contained in F. S. Regs., Part II. and the Staff Manual respectively. Title Pages will be prepared in manuscript.

Place	Date	Hour	Summary of Events and Information	Remarks and references to Appendices
Equancourt	15th		No 2 Section Inspected by B.G., R.A. 31th Division	
	16th		2nd Lt. T.J. LACY R.F.A. of England, Struck off the strength	
	17th		Horse Routine – Supply of Ammunition.	
	18th		No 1 Section began training.	
	19th		2nd Lt. J. N. McLEOD R.F.A. Joined from 173rd Bde. & Posted to No 3 Section	
			" H. Iddon R.F.A. " 173rd Bde. Posted to 173rd Bde.	
	20th		Horse Routine – Supply of Ammunition.	
	21st		do	
	22nd		do	
	23rd		do	
	24th		do	
	25th		do	
	26th		do	
	27th		No 1 Section Completed Period of training	
			No 1 Section Inspected by B.G., R.A. 31th Division and G.O.C., R.A. II Corps.	
	28th		Horse Routine – Supply of Ammunition	
	29th		do	
	30th		do	
	–		Casualties during Month of September:- Nil.	
	1/10			

H.M.W. Lloyd Major R.F.A.
Commander, 31th Divisional Ammunition Column

Army Form C. 2118.

36 D Am Col

Vol 22

WAR DIARY
or
INTELLIGENCE SUMMARY.
(Erase heading not required.)

Place	Date	Hour	Summary of Events and Information	Remarks and references to Appendices
EQUANCOURT	1/9/17		Usual Routine. Supply of Ammunition.	
	2		Inspection by M.G., R.A. 3rd Army.	
	3		G.O.C. 4th Corps.	
	4		Usual Routine Supply of Ammunition.	
	5		do	
	6		do	Capt. R.B.HENNESSEY.(R.A.M.C.) Admitted to Hospital
	7		Capt. J.G.HARVEY. (C.of F.) To England. Struck off the strength.	
	8		Usual Routine.	
	9		Supply of Ammunition.	
	10		do	
	11		do	
	-		No. 3 Section complete Period of training.	
	-		No. 3 Section Inspected by G.O.C., R.A. IV Corps and B.G., R.A., 36th Division.	
	12		2nd/Lt. T.R.WILLIAMS. R.F.A. Admitted to Hospital.	
	13		Capt. R.B.HENNESSEY. R.A.M.C. Rejoined from Hospital.	
	14		Usual Routine Supply of Ammunition.	
	15		do	
	16		do	

WAR DIARY
or
INTELLIGENCE SUMMARY.
(Erase heading not required.)

Army Form C. 2118.

Place	Date	Hour	Summary of Events and Information	Remarks and references to Appendices
ESVANCOURT	17/7/19		Nonac Routine – Supply of Ammunition.	
	18		Capt. C.C. MANNING. (C.E.F.) taken on the strength with effect from 15.7.19.	
	19		Nonac Routine – Supply of Ammunition.	
	20		do	
	21		Lieut. J.L.H. POLLEN. R.F.A. Joins from Base posted to No 2 Section	
	22		Nonac Routine – Supply of Ammunition.	
	23		do	
	24		do	
	25		2○Lieut. W.R. PICKETT. R.F.A. granted permission to wear the Badge of Lieut Anty R.A.D.O. 2220 4.3.7.9	
	26		Nonac Routine – Supply of Ammunition	
	27		do	
	28		2○Lieut T.R. WILLIAMS. R.F.A. Invalided to England – Struck off its Strength with effect from 15.10.19	
	29		Nonac Routine – Supply of Ammunition	
	30		do	
	31		do	
			Casualties during month of October – Nil.	

A.W. Riley Lieut R.A.
Commanding, 37th Divl Amm Column.

Army Form C. 2118.

WAR DIARY
~~INTELLIGENCE SUMMARY~~

(Erase heading not required.)

36th DAC

Place	Date	Hour	Summary of Events and Information	Remarks and references to Appendices
EQUANCOURT	1/4/17		Normal Routine – Supply of Ammunition to Decauville to Battery Positions	
	2/4/17		do	
	3/4/17		do	
	4/4/17		do	
	5/4/17		do	
BARASTRE	6/4/17		Headquarters, No's 1 and 2 Sections Marched to BARASTRE.	
			S.A.A. Section Marched to BEAUVENCOURT.	
	7/4/17		Normal Routine – Supply of Ammunition by Decauville to Battery Positions.	
			Lieut. J.L.H. POLLEN, R.F.A. posted to 36th D.A.C. H.Q.	
	8/4/17		Normal Routine – Supply of Ammunition by Decauville to Battery Positions. Shelled off the strength.	
	9/4/17		do	
	10/4/17		Special Supply of Ammunition – 5040 Rds 18pr by Decauville to Hermies forward Dump	
	11/4/17		do – 5040 " do	
			do – 2520 " do	
			do – 2736 " do	
			do – 576 " 4.5" do	
			do – 4560 " 18pr do	
			do – 172 " 4.5 do	
			do – 3240 " 4.5 by Decauville to Hermies forward Dump (area METZ)	
			do – 180 by Lighter from 60 to Perm Dump to Battery area	
	12/4/17		do – 180 by Lighter from 60 to Perm Dump to Battery area	
	"		do – do	
	"		do – do	
	"		do – do	
	"		do – 4.5 by Decauville to Hermies forward Dump	
	13/4/17		H.Qrs. No's 1, 2 and S.A.A. Section Marched to HAPLINCOURT.	
			Special Supply of Ammunition- 1000 Rds "B" Smoke by Decauville to Hermies forward Dump	
			do – 1080 " "A" Smoke by Decauville to do	
	14/4/17		do – 2420 " "A" do	

WAR DIARY
~~INTELLIGENCE SUMMARY~~
(Erase heading not required.)

Army Form C. 2118.

Place	Date	Hour	Summary of Events and Information	Remarks and references to Appendices
HAPLINCOURT	15/11		Special Supply of Ammunition – 6080 Rds 18 Pdr. H.E. from 500/sq Reserve Dump. 136 Battery H.E. gun.	
			108 do. 810 do. 4·5" H.E. Received & Ammunition Forward Dump.	
	16/11		Pack Section formed from S.A.A. Section under 2nd Lt E.N.P. FISHER, R.F.A.	
			Special Supply of Ammunition – 2240 Rds. 18 Pdr H.E. Pack Ammo. from Hermies Forward Dump	
	17/11		New Forward Dump "PLUM" commenced. 2nd Lt A. STILWELL, R.F.A. in charge. to Battery positions.	
	18/11		Echelon filled up to Establishment with Ammunition	
	19/11		Normal Routine – Supply of Ammunition	
RUYALCOURT	20/11		H.Qs. No.1 am 2 Sections also S.A.A. Sechon marched from HAPLINCOURT to RUYALCOURT.	
	21/11		93rd B.A.C. came under orders of C.O. of this Unit	
	22/11		Normal Routine – Supply of Ammunition. Forward Dump kept up to Establishment of 200 Gr Guns.	
	23/11		do	
	24/11		do	
	25/11		do	
	26/11		do	
	27/11		do	
	28/11		do	
	29/11		do	
	30/11		do. 2nd D.A.C. came under Orders of C.O. of this Unit for Supply of Ammunition. 1 O.R. Wounded & 1 Animal killed by Enemy Shell Fire.	
	30/11		Administration of Ammn. Supply taken over by O.C. 2nd D.A.C. Commde 35th Divisional Ammn Column.	H.W. Coy Major R.F.A. O/C 35th D.A.C.

WAR DIARY
INTELLIGENCE SUMMARY

Army Form C. 2118.

36th Divl. Ammn. Column

Vol 24

Place	Date	Hour	Summary of Events and Information	Remarks and references to Appendices
ROYALCOURT	1/7/17		Usual Routine. Supply of Ammunition.	
	2/7/17		do	
	3/7/17		do	
	4/7/17		A.R.P. and Bomb Section handed over to 2@Divisions.	
	5/7/17		Usual Routine - Supply of Ammunition	
	6/7/17		do	
	7/7/17		Enemy shelled tree Area. Casualties. 1 Mule Killed - 3 Mules destroyed.	
	8/7/17		Usual Routine. Supply of Ammunition	
	9/7/17		do	
	10/7/17		do	
	11/7/17		do	
	12/7/17		do	
	13/7/17		H.Qrs, No.1 & 2 Sections also S.A.A. Section Marched to YTRES.	
	14/7/17		Usual Routine. Supply of Ammunition	
	15/7/17		do	
YTRES	16/7/17		Capt. J.M.H. Fraser, R.F.A. attached to H.Qrs. 36th Divl Artz. 2nd Lt. F.A. Simmonds, R.F.A. to take over duties of Acting Adjutant.	
	17/7/17		Usual Routine. Supply of Ammunition	
			do	

Army Form C. 2118.

WAR DIARY
or
INTELLIGENCE SUMMARY.
(Erase heading not required.)

Place	Date	Hour	Summary of Events and Information	Remarks and references to Appendices
YPRES	18/7/17		Monae Routine - Supply of Ammunition.	
	19/7/17		do	
	20/7/17		2nd Lt. H.V. COURSE R.F.A. taken on the strength with effect from 18/7/17.	
	21/7/17		Monal Routine. Supply of Ammunition.	
	22/7/17		METZ Dump taken over by O.C. of this Unit	
	23/7/17		Monae Routine - Supply of Ammunition	
	24/7/17		do	
	25/7/17		do	
			METZ DUMP handed over to 63rd R.N. Division 26/7/17.	
	26/7/17		H.Os, 76 & 172 also 199A Echon Marched from YPRES to BEAULENCOURT.	
BEAULENCOURT	27/7/17		This Unit camped at BEAULENCOURT awaiting orders.	
	28/7/17		do	
	29/7/17		do	
	30/7/17		do	
	31/7/17		do	
			CASUALTIES:- Officers NIL ORs NIL.	

R.M. Kay? Lt Col
Comdg 31 D.A.C.

Army Form C. 2118.

36th D.A.C.

VII 25

WAR DIARY
or
INTELLIGENCE SUMMARY.

(Erase heading not required.)

Place	Date	Hour	Summary of Events and Information	Remarks and references to Appendices
BEAULENCOURT.	1/1/8		HQrs, No 1 + 2, also S.A.A Section marched to DERNANCOURT.	A/F
	2/1/8		do do VAIRE.	A/F
VAIRE	3/1/8		2nd/Lt. W.J. JEANS R.F.A. taken on the strength and posted to No 2 Section.	A/F
	4/1/8		" G.F. HALLETT R.F.A. do do 1 "	A/F
	5/1/8		This Unit Camped at VAIRE awaiting orders.	A/F
	6/1/8		do	A/F
	7/1/8		HQrs, No 1 + 2 also S.A.A Section marched to HANGEST en SANTERRE.	A/F
HANGEST.	8/1/8		This Unit Camped at HANGEST awaiting orders.	A/F
	9/1/8		No 1 Section marched from HANGEST to SOLENTE	A/F
	10/1/8		No 1 Section " " SOLENTE to HAPPENCOURT.	A/F
	—		Capt. G.G. MANNING Bg?? attached to this Unit awarded the Military Cross. See BATO 223	A/F
	11/1/8		HQrs, No 2 + S.A.A Section marched from HANGEST to ROYE	A/F
	12/1/8		The HQrs No 2 + S.M Section camped at ROYE awaiting Orders.	A/F
	13/1/8		HQrs, No 2 + S.A.A Section marched from ROYE to DURY.	A/F
DURY	14/1/8		Usual Routine. Supply of Ammunition	A/F
	15/1/8		do	A/F
	16/1/8		do ———— Spinning Dump taken over from DURY to St SIMON.	A/F
	17/1/8		HQrs, No 2 + S.A.A Section marched from SEREAUCOURT to St SIMON.	A/F
	"		No 1 Section marched from SEREAUCOURT to St SIMON	A/F
St SIMON			St SIMON Dump taken over by O.C. of this Unit.	A/F

Army Form C. 2118.

WAR DIARY
or
INTELLIGENCE SUMMARY.
(Erase heading not required.)

Instructions regarding War Diaries and Intelligence Summaries are contained in F. S. Regs., Part II. and the Staff Manual respectively. Title pages will be prepared in manuscript.

Place	Date	Hour	Summary of Events and Information	Remarks and references to Appendices
St Simon	17/8		2nd Lieut E.M.P. Fisher. RFA admitted to Hospital.	A/R
	18/8		Usual Routine – Supply of Ammunition.	A/R
	19/8		do	A/R
	20/8		do	A/R
	21/8		do	A/R
	22/8		do	A/R
	23/8		do	A/R
	24/8		do	A/R
	25/8		Lieut W.R. Parbury. RFA taken on the strength of this Unit. Posted to S.A.A. Section.	A/R
	"		Capt F.W.H. Magee. RFA ceases to be attached to HQrs 36 Div Arty.	A/R
	26/8		Usual Routine – Supply of Ammn. – Indian Personel joined this Unit	A/R
	27/8		do	A/R
	28/8		do	A/R
	29/8		do	A/R
	30/8		do	A/R
	31/8		do	A/R
	-		Casualties to Officers & O.R.'s during the month :- Nil Animals :- Nil	
	-		Lieut Col. J.H.G. Riley. RFA & Capt F.W.H. Magee RFA mentioned in Despatches. London Gazette	A/R
	31/8		A.K. Riley Lieut Col RFA Commanding 36th Divisional Ammn Column

Army Form C. 2118.

WAR DIARY
INTELLIGENCE SUMMARY

(Erase heading not required.)

36 D Amm Col

Vol 26

Place	Date	Hour	Summary of Events and Information	Remarks and references to Appendices
St Simon	1/7/8		Usual Routine – Supply & Ammunition.	n/g
	2/7/8		do	n/g
	3/7/8		do	n/g
	4/7/8		do	n/g
	5/7/8		do	n/g
	6/7/8		do	n/g
	7/7/8		Right forward Dump taken over by OC of this Unit	n/g
	8/7/8		do " " " " " "	n/g
	9/7/8		Left " " " " " "	n/g
	10/7/8		do " " " " " "	n/g
	11/7/8		do	n/g
	12/7/8		do	n/g
	13/7/8		do	n/g
	14/7/8		do	n/g
	15/7/8		do	n/g
	16/7/8		do	n/g
	17/7/8		do	n/g

Army Form C. 2118.

WAR DIARY
or
INTELLIGENCE SUMMARY.
(Erase heading not required.)

Instructions regarding War Diaries and Intelligence Summaries are contained in F. S. Regs., Part II. and the Staff Manual respectively. Title pages will be prepared in manuscript.

Place	Date	Hour	Summary of Events and Information	Remarks and references to Appendices
St Simon	18/7/18		2nd Lt. G.F. HALLETT. R.F.A. admitted to Hospital.	ng
	19/7/18		Horse Routine — Supply of Ammunition.	ng
	20/7/18		2nd Lt. E.M.P. FISHER. R.F.A. invalided to England on the 23/7/18, & struck off the Strength	ng
	21/7/18		Major. W. GRAHAM. R.F.A. assumes Command of the Unit on Lt. Col. T.H.G. RILEY. R.F.A. proceeding on leave	ng
	22/7/18		Normal Routine — Supply of Ammunition	ng
	23/7/18		do	ng
	24/7/18		do	ng
	25/7/18		do	ng
	26/7/18		do	ng
	27/7/18		do	ng
	28/7/18		Casualties to Officers & OR's during the month:- Nil. Animals:- Nil.	ng

28/7/1918.

W. Graham. Major R.F.A.
Commanding, 36th Divisional Ammunition Column.

36th Divisional Artillery.

36th DIVISIONAL AMMUNITION COLUMN R.F.A.

MARCH   1918

WAR DIARY
~~INTELLIGENCE SUMMARY~~
(Erase heading not required.)

Army Form C. 2118.

36" T.A.C.

Place	Date	Hour	Summary of Events and Information	Remarks and references to Appendices
ST SIMON	1/3/18		Improving horse standings and erecting splinter proof walls around billets & horse standings. Cultivating land for vegetable production. Supply of Ammunition to Battery Wagon Lines, also kept forward dumps at La Fontaine and Epehy up to an establishment of 4000 Rds 18 Pr and 600 Rds 4.5 How. Dumped at Rear Battle Positions 800 Rds per Gun. Party of 116 OR's detailed daily for building Gun Pits in Battle Positions.	
	2/3/18		do	
	3/3/18		do	
	4/3/18		do	
	5/3/18		do	
	6/3/18		do	
	7/3/18		do	
	8/3/18		do	
	9/3/18		do	
	10/3/18		do	
	11/3/18		do	
	12/3/18		do	
	13/3/18		do	

2/Lieut. G.F. HALLETT. R.F.A. rejoined from Hospital.

Army Form C. 2118.

WAR DIARY
or
INTELLIGENCE SUMMARY.
(Erase heading not required.)

Instructions regarding War Diaries and Intelligence Summaries are contained in F. S. Regs., Part II. and the Staff Manual respectively. Title pages will be prepared in manuscript.

Place	Date	Hour	Summary of Events and Information	Remarks and references to Appendices
ST SIMION	14/8		Improving Horse Standings and erecting Shelter, Drop Walls around Billets and Horse Standings	N/R
	"		Cultivating Land for Vegetable Growing	N/R
	"		Supply of Ammunition to Battery Wagon Lines, also kept forward Dumps at La Fontaine and Caote up to an establishment of 4000 Rds 18Pr and 600 Rds 4.5 How.	N/R
	"		Dumps at Rear Battle Positions 800 Rds per Gun 18Pr in Battle Positions.	N/R
	15/8		Party of 116 OR's details daily for building Gun Pits in Battle Positions.	N/R
	16/8		do	N/R
	17/8		do	N/R
	18/8		do	N/R
	19/8		Enemy Bombed Advan Dumps and Horse Lines. Casualties Nil	N/R
	20/8		Enemy Shelled this Area. Casualties 2. ORs Wounded.	N/R
	21/8		HQrs No 1-2 + SAA Sections marched with full Echelons to SOMETTE EAUCOURT.	N/R
SOMETTE.EAUCOURT.	"		Camp shelled by Enemy. Casualties Nil.	N/R
VERLAINES	"		HQrs No 1-2 + SAA Echelons marched with full Echelons to VERLAINES.	N/R
FRETOY.le.CHATEAU	22/8		HQrs No 1 + 2 Sections marched from VERLAINES to FRETOY le Chateau.	N/R
	"		Dumps established at FRENICHES and GUISCARD	N/R
	"		SAA Section marched with full Echelon from VERLAINES to FLAN le Martelesse to keep up supply of S.A.A. to Infantry.	N/R

WAR DIARY
or
INTELLIGENCE SUMMARY.
(Erase heading not required.)

Instructions regarding War Diaries and Intelligence Summaries are contained in F.S. Regs., Part II. and the Staff Manual respectively. Title pages will be prepared in manuscript.

Place	Date	Hour	Summary of Events and Information	Remarks and references to Appendices
FRETOY le CHATEAU	23/3/18		No1 Section, 20th D.A.C. also D/232 Bde. 463@Bty, A.B.C. Rations (Wagon Lines) 173@Bde. R.F.A. came under orders of O.C. of this unit.	
"	"		H.Qrs. No1 + 2 Sections marched from FRETOY le CHATEAU to AVRICOURT.	
AVRICOURT.	"		S.A.A. Section rejoined at AVRICOURT and marched out same night with Infantry Dump's established. A.R.P. at X Roads between AVRICOURT and BEAULIU.	
"	24/3/18		Forward Dumps. at BEAULIU, les FONTAINES and MUIRANCOURT.	
FRESNIERES	25/3/18		H.Qrs. No1 + 2 Sections marched from AVRICOURT to FRESNIERES where Dumps established.	H.R.
ORVILLERS	26/3/18		do FRESNIERES to ORVILLERS and Refir up supply of Ammunition to Forward Dumps at MARGNY-SUR-MATZ and MAREUIL LAMOTTE from A.R.P. established at RESSONS.	H.R.
"	"		H.Qrs. No1 + 2 Sections marched for ORVILLERS to MERY and Keft up supply of Ammunition to MAREIUL LAMOTTE.	H.R.
MERY.	27/3/18		O.C. this Unit became responsible for supply of Rations & Forage to Divisional Artillery and all attached Units, drawing from Recus Dump at RESSONS and delivering to Units	
"	"		H.Qrs. No1 + 2 Sections marched from MERY to GOURNAY & Kept up supply of Ammn & Rations.	H.R.
GOURNAY.	28/3/18		Special Supply of Ammunition also Rations & Forage.	H.R.
GRAND FRESNOY.	29/3/18 30/3/18		H.Qrs. No1 + 2 Sections marched from GOURNAY to Grand FRESNOY.	H.R.

Army Form C. 2118.

WAR DIARY
or
INTELLIGENCE SUMMARY.
(Erase heading not required.)

Instructions regarding War Diaries and Intelligence Summaries are contained in F. S. Regs., Part II and the Staff Manual respectively. Title pages will be prepared in manuscript.

Place	Date	Hour	Summary of Events and Information	Remarks and references to Appendices
GRAND FRESNOY.	30/3/18		A.B.C. Batteries (Magazine) 193 able to D/282 RFA ceased to be functional by mo.	RFA RFA
LA RUE ST PIERRE.	31/3/18		Hdq. No-1 & 2 Sections marched from GRAND FRESNOY to LA RUE ST PIERRE.	RFA

Total casualties for month.

Officers. NIL
O.R's. 2 Wounded.
Animals. NIL

A.H.Riley Lt Col R.F.A.
Commanding "36 Divisional Ammunition Column

5/4/1918.

36th Divisional Artillery.

36th DIVISIONAL AMMUNITION COLUMN R.F.A. ::: APRIL 1918.

WAR DIARY
or
INTELLIGENCE SUMMARY.

Army Form C. 2118.

36 D Am Col

Vol 28

Place	Date	Hour	Summary of Events and Information	Remarks and references to Appendices
LA RUE ST PIERRE	1/7/18		Normal Routine – supply of Ammunition.	
AUCHY-la-MONTAGNE	2/7/18	4.19p.	Nos 1 + 2 Echons also D.H. Personnel marched to AUCHY LA MONTAGNE. CHARMES.	
CHARMES	3/7/18		do	
	4/7/18		Awaiting Orders & refitting Sections.	
	5/7/18		No 1 Section 20th D.A.C. closed to be functioned by us & reopened as our own unit. Awaiting Orders & refitting Sections.	
	6/7/18		do	
	7/7/18		do	
COURCELLES	8/7/18	7.19p.	Nos 1 + 2 Echons also D.H. Personnel marched to COURCELLES. V. 184 heavy march horse to D/232 Bde scout to be functioned by us.	
	9/7/18		Awaiting Orders.	
	10/7/18		do	
Pont de Metz	11/7/18	1.19p.	Nos 1 + 2 Sections also D.H. Personnel marched to PONT-de-METZ.	
	12/7/18		Awaiting Orders	
	13/7/18		do	
	14/7/18		Nos 1 + 2 Sections also D.H. Personnel marched to St Roch Salin Dep transit for HOSPITAL Siding	
HOSPITAL MONT des CATS	15/7/18		Arrived at HOSPITRE SIDING & Personnel marched to MONT des CATS	
	16/7/18	7.19p	Nos 1 + 2 Sections also D.H. Personnel marched to GODAWAERSVELDE.	
GODAWAERSVELDE	17/7/18	12.24p.m	Ex. Returned to march Batt'y Dump	
	18/7/18	4.56 p.m	18 P'dr. + 4.5' Mors to Battery Position at 158 J.1.3 Bde IAA.	
	19/7/18	10.9/18	2nd Lt. M.F. PARBURY R.F.A. awarded MILITARY CROSS	

WAR DIARY or INTELLIGENCE SUMMARY

Army Form C. 2118.

Place	Date	Hour	Summary of Events and Information	Remarks and references to Appendices
GODEWAERSVELDE	19/4/18		2nd Lt. G. ISMAY, R.F.A., 2nd Lt. F.C. JARVIS, R.F.A. & 2nd Lt. G.F. HALLETT, R.F.A. to 153 Bde. for duty.	
"	20/4		Awaiting Orders.	
"	21/4		MAJOR W. GRAHAM, R.F.A. proceeded to England & struck off the strength. Awaiting Orders.	
"	22/4		do	
"	23/4		do	
"	24/4		M.O.S. No.1 + 2 Sections + Other Personnel marched to HAYHOEK STANDINGS.	
HAYHOEK PESELHOEK	25/4		3rd L.D. Private KELL in the line of march by Enemy Rifle fire. M.O.S. No.1 + 2 Sections + Ammunition marched to PESELHOEK STANDINGS.	
"	26/4/18		Lieut. F.A. PRICE, M.C., R.F.A. looks from 153 Bde. R.F.A. to Command No.1 Section and to be Acting Captain whilst so employed with effect from 26-4-18 Auth. R320 24.4.18 dated. P.A. Dunch came under orders at O.C. of this Unit. 480 Rds. B x delivered to D/173 Bde. Ammn delivered to Batteries 238 Rds. to A/153 Bde — 152 Rds. to B/153 Bde — D/173 Bde. — A/153 Bde —	
"	27/4		2nd Lt. G. ISMAY R.F.A. reported from 153 Bde R.F.A. 14th Rds to D/173 Bde.	
"	28/4		488 Rds A/153 Bde — 720 Rds to D/153 Bde. Ammn delivered to Batteries.	
"	29/4		2nd Lt. F.E. LEVI, R.F.A. to Kemper the strength Posted to No.1 Section.	
"	30/4			

Total Casualties for month — OFFICERS. O.Rs ANIMALS.
Nil — 2 Wounded — 2 Killed —

A. Riley
Comdg. 3rd Divisional Amm.n Colmn.

WAR DIARY or INTELLIGENCE SUMMARY

Army Form C. 2118.

36th D.A.C.

Vol 24

Place	Date	Hour	Summary of Events and Information	Remarks and references to Appendices
PESELHOEK	1/5/18		2/Lieut F. LEYL RFA taken on the strength and posted to No 2 Section	AAR
	"		Ammunition supply by Decauville to Batteries from P.A. Dump	AA5
	2/5/18		Lieut R.B. NUNN M.C. RFA taken on the strength of H.Q. Station attached to 2nd Supp. H.Q.	AA6
	"		Ammunition supply to Batteries by 19.000 sets from P.A. Dump	
	3/5/18		do	
	"		One Light Draught Horse killed by enemy shell fire	
	4/5/18		One OR wounded & One Light Draught Horse killed by enemy shell fire	
	"		One Light Draught Horse wounded by enemy shell fire	
	5/5/18		Ammunition supply by Decauville to Batteries from P.A. Dump	
	6/5/18		do	
	7/5/18		do	
	"		Lieut D.Y. WHEATLEY RFA Admitted to Hospital sick	
	8/5/18		Ammunition supply by Decauville to Batteries from P.A. Dump	
	9/5/18		Lieut W.F. PARBURY M.C. RFA attached to 153rd Bde for duty	
	"		Ammunition supply by Decauville to Batteries from P.A. Dump	
	10/5/18		Ammunition taken in charge BCBR. however FPS 266 rd from "B" Corps.	
	11/5/18		A.D.2 Section moved from PESELHOEK to HAMHOEK	
	"		Ammunition supply by Decauville to Batteries from P.A. Dump	

Army Form C. 2118.

WAR DIARY
or
INTELLIGENCE SUMMARY.
(Erase heading not required.)

Place	Date	Hour	Summary of Events and Information	Remarks and references to Appendices
HAMHOEK	12/5/18		HQrs & No 1 Section marched from PESELHOEK to HAMHOEK standings.	
	13/5/18		Ammunition supply by Decauville to Batteries from P.A Dump.	
	14/5/18		2/Lieut A. STILWELL R.F.A. attached to 153rd Bde for duty.	
	15/5/18		One OR Wounded & One mule killed by Enemy Shelling	
	16/5/18		Improving Horse Standings & Erecting Splinter Proof Walls around Billets Horse standings	
	17/5/18		do	
	18/5/18		Capt F.W.H. MAGEE R.F.A. attached to 153rd Bde as Adjutant. 2/Lt SIMMONS R.F.A takes over	
	19/5/18		2/Lieut C.H. VAUGHAN INNIS. FUS. attached to S.A.A. Section for duty	
	20/5/18		Usual Routine - Erecting Splinter Proof Walls around Billets Horse Standings	
	21/5/18		do	
	22/5/18		Ammunition drawn from HENDERSON DUMP vice hazards OX to complete Establishment	
	23/5/18		Lieut W.F. PARBURY M.C. R.F.A. posted to 153rd Bde 23rd May 1918.	
	23/5/18		2/Lieut P. CALLENDER R.F.A. posted to No 1 Section 23.5.18.	
	25/5/18		Lieut DYNWHEATLEY R.F.A. evacuated to England 15.5.18.	
	26/5/18		Usual Routine - Erecting Splinter Proof Walls around Billets Horse Standing	
	27/5/18		4 OR's Wounded to Duma & Lne by Enemy Shell Fire	
	28/5/18		Usual Routine - Erecting Helmlet Proof Walls around Billets Horse Standings	
			Capt F.W.H. MAGEE R.F.A. proceeded from 153rd Bde & Resumed duties as Adjutant	
	29/5/18		Usual Routine - Erecting Splinter Proof Walls around Billets Horse Standings	
	30/5/18		Ammunition supply by Decauville to Batteries from P.A. Dump	
	31/5/18		do	

Total casualties for Month: Officers Nil, 6 Wounded 9 Killed 1 Wounded (remained on duty) 30th from Bn 1

Army Form C. 2118.

36 D Aus Col

Vol 30

WAR DIARY
or
INTELLIGENCE SUMMARY.
(Erase heading not required.)

Instructions regarding War Diaries and Intelligence Summaries are contained in F.S. Regs., Part II. and the Staff Manual respectively. Title pages will be prepared in manuscript.

Place	Date	Hour	Summary of Events and Information	Remarks and references to Appendices
HANHOEK	1/9/18		Musar Pondros. Erecting Splinter proof - mens Quarters. Billets found to out to	
	2/9/18		2/Lt C. CHRISTIE. Rgt take. on Establishment to Bns.	
	3/9/18		Men at fatigue-duties cleaning Camp. Also cleaning Rifles and the Horses.	
	4/9/18		do	
	5/9/18		do	
	6/9/18		do	
	7/9/18		do	
	8/9/18		NOP. No 1 + 2 & sections proceed from HANHOEK to PONTNYA Camp.	
	9/9/18		NOP. No 1 + 2 at SAA Section inspected by G.O.C. II Bde.	
	10/9/18		NOP. No 1 2 + SAA Section commence training	
	11/9/18		do	
	12/9/18		do	
	13/9/18		do	
	14/9/18		do	
	15/9/18		do	
	16/9/18		NOP No 1, 2 + SAA Sections inspected by G.O.C. RA II Div.	
	17/9/18		Lieut N.J.B. PITT. Rey Saxon on the strength of No 2 Sec. with effect from 11/9/18.	
PONTNYA CAMP.	18/9/18		NOP. No 1, 2 + SAA Sections undergoing course of training	
	19/9/18		do	

Army Form C. 2118.

WAR DIARY
or
INTELLIGENCE SUMMARY.
(Erase heading not required.)

Instructions regarding War Diaries and Intelligence Summaries are contained in F. S. Regs., Part II. and the Staff Manual respectively. Title pages will be prepared in manuscript.

Place	Date	Hour	Summary of Events and Information	Remarks and references to Appendices
PONTYPOOL CAMP.	20/8		HQrs, No 1, 2 & S.A.A. Section undergoing Course of Training	AHS
	21/8		do	AHS
	22/8		do	AHS
	23/8		Lieut. I. PIERCE. 9th R. Innis. Fus. joined to undergo course as Staff Learner.	AHS
	24/8		HQrs, No 1, 2 & S.A.A. Section undergoing course of training	AHS
	25/8		do	AHS
	26/8		do	AHS
	27/8		Lieut I. PIERCE, 9th R. Innis. Fus. Ceased to be attached to this Unit.	AHS
	28/8		HQrs, No 1, 2 & S.A.A. Sections undergoing course of training.	AHS
	29/8		do	AHS
	30/8		do	AHS
	31/8		Total Casualties to Personnel & Animals :— Nil.	AHS

A. Wilson Lieut. D.A.C.
Commdg. 36th Divisional Ammunition Column.

WAR DIARY or INTELLIGENCE SUMMARY

Army Form C. 2118.

36th DAC

Place	Date	Hour	Summary of Events and Information	Remarks and references to Appendices
PONT/POOL CAMP	1/7/18		H.Qrs. No 1, 2 & S.A.A. Sections undergoing Course of training.	R/R
	2/7/18		do	R/R
	3/7/18		Lieut. R.B. NUNN, R.F.A. posted from No 1 Section to 30th Divisional Artillery	R/R
	4/7/18		H.Qrs. No 1, 2 + S.A.A. Sections marched to ZERMEZEELE Area.	R/R
ZERMEZEELE	5/7/18		Awaiting Orders	R/R
	6/7/18		Dump established at BELFORT 2. 27/R.7.a.55	R/R
	7/7/18		do	R/R
ST SYLVESTRE CAPPEL	8/7/18		H.Qrs. No 1 + 2 Sections marched to ST SYLVESTRE CAPPEL area.	R/R
	"		Ammn. delivered to Batteries:- 228 Bde 183r to 153 Bde = 228 Bde 183r to 173 Bde } by	R/R
	"	9am	do 228 Bde 183r to 153 Bde = 288 Bde 4/5 to 173 Bde } force	R/R
	"		do 228 Bde 160r to 173 Bde = do } Transport	R/R
	9/7/18		do 684 Bde "A" Store to 173 Bde	R/R
	"		S.A.A. Section marched to ST SYLVESTRE CAPPEL area	R/R
	"		Ammn. delivered to Batteries:- 304 Bde "A" Smoke to HQ A.F.A Bde, 300 Bde "A" Smoke to 173 Bde.	R/R
	10/7/18		do 456 Bde 183r to 153 Bde 576 Bde 4/5 to 153 Bde	R/R
EECKE	11/7/18		H.Qrs. No 1 + 2 Sections marched to EECKE Area.	R/R
	12/7/18		Ordinary Daily Routine	R/R
	13/7/18		do	R/R
	14/7/18		do	R/R

Army Form C. 2118.

WAR DIARY
or
INTELLIGENCE SUMMARY.

(Erase heading not required.)

Instructions regarding War Diaries and Intelligence Summaries are contained in F. S. Regs., Part II. and the Staff Manual respectively. Title pages will be prepared in manuscript.

Place	Date	Hour	Summary of Events and Information	Remarks and references to Appendices
EECKE	15/8		Ordinary Daily Routine.	
	16/8		do	
	17/8		do	
	18/8		Ammn delivered to Batteries :– 300 Rds "B" Smke to D/153 Bde = 300 Rds B Smoke D/153 Bde } by	
	19/8		do 400 Rds TMG to 36th DTMO	horse
	"		do 1824 Rds 18pr to 153 CBde = 384 Rds 4.5 to 153 CBde } transport.	
	"		do 451 " 18pr to 173 PBde = 192 Rds 4.5 to 173 PBde	
	20/8		Ordinary Daily Routine.	
	21/8		do	
	"		Ammn delivered to Batteries :– 1520 Rds 18pr to 153 CBde = 684 Rds 18pr + 288 Rds 4.5 to 153 PBde } horse	
	"		288 " 4.5 to 153 PBde = 300 Rds TMG to 36th DTMO } transport	
	22/8		Ammn delivered to Batteries :– 760 Rds 18pr to 153 PBde, also 192 Rds 4.5 to 153 PBde	
	"		836 " 18pr + 96 Rds 4.5 to 173 PBde.	
	23/8		Ammn delivered to Batteries :– 300 Rds T.M.G. delivered to 36th D.T.M.O.	
	24/8		Ordinary Daily Routine :– 100 " " "	
	25/8		Ammn delivered to Batteries :– 456 Rds 18pr to 173 PBde	
	26/8		Ordinary Daily Routine.	
	27/8		do	
	28/8		do 96th B.A.C. came under the Orders of O.C. of this Unit.	
	29/8		Ammn delivered to Batteries :– 826 Rds 18pr + 192 Rds 4.5 to 173 PBde.	

Army Form C. 2118.

WAR DIARY
or
INTELLIGENCE SUMMARY.
(Erase heading not required.)

Instructions regarding War Diaries and Intelligence Summaries are contained in F. S. Regs., Part II. and the Staff Manual respectively. Title pages will be prepared in manuscript.

Place	Date	Hour	Summary of Events and Information	Remarks and references to Appendices
EECKE	29/7/18		Ammn delivered :— 100 Rds T.M.G. to D.T.M.O.	AHR
	30/7/18		—"— 144 Rds B.N.C. to D/153 Bde 144 Rds B.N.C. to D/173 Bde.	AHR
	31/7/18		Ordinary Daily Routine	AHR
			Total Casualties to Personnel and Animals :— Nil.	AHR

31/7/18.

A. Wiley Lieut Col. R.F.A.
Commanding, 36th Divisional Ammunition Column

WAR DIARY or INTELLIGENCE SUMMARY.

Army Form C.2118.

36 D Am Col

Vol 32

Place	Date	Hour	Summary of Events and Information	Remarks and references to Appendices
EECKE	1/8/18		Ammunition delivered to Batteries:- 300 Rds. T.M.G. to D.T.M.O.	AAA
	2/8/18		2nd Lieut. C.H.VAUGHAN. Inns. Fus. ceased to be attached on rejoining 36th Bn. M.G. Corps.	AAA
	3/8/18		Ordinary Daily Routine. Hauling R.E. Material to Battery positions	AAA
	4/8/18		do do	AAA
	5/8/18		Ammunition delivered:- 600 Rds. T.M.G. to D.T.M.O.	AAA
	6/8/18		Ordinary Daily Routine. Hauling R.E. Material to Battery positions	AAA
	7/8/18		No.2 Section moved from Sheet 27/Q.25.d.8.3. to Sheet 27/Q.25.a.75.95	AAA
	8/8/18		Ordinary Daily Routine. Hauling R.E. material to Battery Sections	AAA
	9/8/18		do	AAA
	10/8/18		Ammunition delivered:- 200 Rds T.M.G. to D.T.M.O.	AAA
	11/8/18		Ordinary Daily Routine. Hauling R.E. Material to Battery positions	AAA
	12/8/18		do	AAA
	13/8/18		do	AAA
	14/8/18		do	AAA
	15/8/18		do	AAA
	16/8/18		Ammunition delivered:- 1400 Rds A.S. from 35th D.T. to Depot Dump.	AAA
	17/8/18		Ordinary Daily Routine. Hauling R.E. material to Battery positions	AAA
	18/8/18		do	AAA
	19/8/18		Lieut. A.A.DEIGHTON. I.A.R. taken on the strength posted to S.A.A. Section.	AAA
	20/8/18		Ammunition delivered:- 200 Rds T.M.G. to D.T.M.O	AAA

WAR DIARY
or
INTELLIGENCE SUMMARY.
(Erase heading not required.)

Army Form C. 2118.

Place	Date	Hour	Summary of Events and Information	Remarks and references to Appendices
EECKE	21/8		Ammunition delivered :- 1400 Rds A.S from 35.⁵ DA to Belfort 2. Dump.	A/R
	22/8		— do — :— 1460 " A.S. "	A/R
	23/8		Ammunition delivered :- 456 Rds A - 284 Rds B.S. to 173 Bde. 604 Rds B.S. from 35.⁵ DA. to Belfort 2 Dump	A/R
	24/8		2⁰ Lieut M.J.B. PITT. RFA posted from No.2. Section to 153 Bde RFA	A/R
			Ammn delivered to Batteries:- 368. 288 to 153 Bde. 456-298 to 173 Bde. 364 and 2B/157 + B/159 Bde	A/R
	25/8		Ordinary Daily Routine. Hauling R.E. material to Battery Positions	A/R
	26/8		do	A/R
	27/8		Casualties by Enemy Shell Fire:- 1 OR. Killed. 1 OR wounded. 5 Mules Killed 3 Mules Wounded	A/R
	28/8		Ordinary Daily Routine. Hauling R.E. material to Battery Positions	A/R
	29/8		do	A/R
	30/8		do	A/R
	31/8		HQrs, No.1 & 2 Sections moved to GODERSVELDE area.	A/R
			Total Casualties during month :- OFFICERS. O.R.ˢ ANIMALS.	A/R
			NIL Killed 1 Wounded 1 Killed 5 Wounded 3	
			1/9/8.	

A Wiley Capt R.F.A.
Commdg. 36th Divisional Ammunition Column

WAR DIARY or INTELLIGENCE SUMMARY.

Army Form C. 2118.

36 D Aux CA

No 33

Place	Date	Hour	Summary of Events and Information	Remarks and references to Appendices
GODEWAERS-VELDE	1/8		Dump Established at ST JANS CAPPEL. S.A.A. Schon moved to BERTHEN. AREA.	
	2/8		Collected Fixed & unfixed Ammunition from 6th Battery Positions. HQs No.1&2. Sections also 96.BAC. marched from Gode. area to SCHAEXKEN area. Ammunition delivered:- 1368 = 288 to 155Bde = 2236 Rds = 576 Rds to 173 Bde	
SCHAEXKEN	3/8		Dump established at DUKE & YORKS SIDING. Ammunition collected from 6th Battery Positions & delivered to ST JANS CAPPEL Dump. Ammunition delivered:- 2052 Rds 136 Rds to 153 Bde.	
	4/8		Dump established at TRESCOTT HOUSE. Ammunition collected from 6th Battery Positions, and delivered to Forward Dumps	
	5/8		Ammunition collected from 6th Battery Positions, and delivered to Forward Dumps. 240 Rds BX delivered to D/153 Bde.	
	6/8		Before No.2. Dump taken over by X Corps. Ammn collected from 6th Battery Positions & delivered to Forward Dumps Dump established at Shed 28 M.34. d. 1. 8.	
			Dump at ST JANS CAPPEL closed.	
	7/8		Ammn collected from ST JANS CAPPEL Dump & delivered M.34. d. 1.8.	
			" " 6th Bty Positions & delivered to M.34. d. 8. 1.	

WAR DIARY
or
INTELLIGENCE SUMMARY.
(Erase heading not required.)

Army Form C. 2118.

Place	Date	Hour	Summary of Events and Information	Remarks and references to Appendices
SCHAEXKEN	7/1/18		Ammunition delivered to Bdes:- A Bx 456 Rds 288 to 173 CRA.	R/R
	8/1/18		96 BAC. ceased to be functioned by OC of this Unit Enemy bombed this Area. Casualties 5. Killed. 9 Wounded. 58. Killed. 19 Wounded.	A/R
	"		Ammunition collected from ST JANS CAPPEL & delivered to PRESCOTT HOUSE & M3rd d. R.D. 336 Rds. 265 T.52 CRds. 288 Rds to 173 CRA.	
	"		Ammunition collected for old positions of 35th D.A. & returned to Depot Dump.	A/R
	9/1/18		No 2 Section moved to R.35.C.6.5. from X 5.c.6.1.	A/R
	"		Ammunition collected from old positions of L.35.S.A. 153@How.RFA.	A/R
	10/1/18		HQr. moved from SCHAEXKEN area to M.25.d.40.40. Ammunition cleared from old positions of 35th D.A. Stokes Mortar Ammunition cleared from old positions.	A/R
	11/1/18		No.2. Section moved from R.35.C.6.5. to M.26.b. 20.25. Amm. delivered to Bdes:- Bx 288 Rds to D/153CRds.	A/R
	12/1/18		" Casualties caused by Enemy Shell fire:- 1 OR Killed 2 ORs Killed 2 mules Killed	A/R
	13/1/18		Ammunition collected from old Battery Positions Ammunition delivered to Bdes:- 288 Rds. Bx to D/153 CRds.	A/R

WAR DIARY
or
INTELLIGENCE SUMMARY

Army Form C. 2118.

Place	Date	Hour	Summary of Events and Information	Remarks and references to Appendices
ST JANS CAPPEL	14/9/18		Collecting Ammunition from Old Battery Positions	AAP
	15/9/18		No.1. Section moved to Sheet 27/R.30.C.4.9.	AAP
	"		Collecting Ammunition from Old Battery Positions	
	"		R.A. Material Dump at TRESCOTT Farm taken over by O.C. of this Unit.	AAP
	16/9/18		2/Lieut. D.A. SMITH R.F.A. Posted to 153rd Bde R.F.A. from No.2 Section.	AAP
	17/9/18		E. F. BRADFORD R.F.A. taken on the strength of No.2 Section from 153rd Bde R.F.A.	AAP
	18/9/18		Hauling R.E. Material to Batteries of 1.30 Bde R.F.A.	AAP
			Ordinary Daily Routine - Erection of Horse Standings.	AAP
			do	AAP
	19/9/18		M.34.d.8.1. Dump to Prescott House Dump handed over to 30th D.A.	AAP
	20/9/18		Capt. J.O. GUERTIN A.V.C. and 2/Lt. H.V. COURSE R.F.A. Admitted to Hospital	AAP
	21/9/18		No.1. Section marched to HAANDEKOT Orchard and surrender orders of GBA 9th Division	AAP
	"		2 Section marched to BUSSEBOOM " " " " " " " 33rd "	AAP
	22/9/18		H.Q. + S.A.A. Section marched to WORMHOUDT area	AAP
WORMHOUDT	23/9/18		Awaiting orders	AAP
	24/9/18		do	AAP
	25/9/18		do	AAP
	26/9/18		do	AAP
	27/9/18		149th & S.A.A. Section marched to ST JAN TER BIEZEN area.	AAP

Army Form C. 2118.

WAR DIARY
or
INTELLIGENCE SUMMARY.
(Erase heading not required.)

Instructions regarding War Diaries and Intelligence Summaries are contained in F. S. Regs., Part II. and the Staff Manual respectively. Title pages will be prepared in manuscript.

Place	Date	Hour	Summary of Events and Information	Remarks and references to Appendices
ST JAN TER BIEZEN	28/9		H.Qrs and S.A.A. Section marched to Dirty Bucket Corner "D" Camp.	AVR
"	29/9		No. 1 & 2 Sections ceased to be functioned by the 9th & 55th D.A.C.	AVR
			S.A.A. Section marched to BRIELEN Area.	AVR
			H.Qrs. marched to VLAMERTINGHE Area.	AVR
VLAMERTINGHE	30/9		Forward Dumps established at Sh 28/ I.9.d & K.14.d.	AVR
			OFFICERS. O.Rs. ANIMALS.	AVR
			KILLED WOUNDED KILLED WOUNDED	AVR
			Nil 6 9 60 19	
			Total casualties during month :—	
	30/9		2 Lieut G. ISMAN. R.F.A. proceeded to R.Stand and struck off the strength with effect from Today.	AVR

A.V. Riley
Lieut R.F.A.
Commanding, 36th Divnl Ammn. Column.

30/9/1918.

2 6 th Mas 95
by Rue?

36th D.A.C.

Vol 34

WAR DIARY
or
INTELLIGENCE SUMMARY.
(Erase heading not required.)

Army Form C. 2118.

Instructions regarding War Diaries and Intelligence Summaries are contained in F.S. Regs., Part II. and the Staff Manual respectively. Title pages will be prepared in manuscript.

Place	Date	Hour	Summary of Events and Information	Remarks and references to Appendices
VLAMER-TINGhE.	1/9/18		Ammunition delivered to Forward Dumps.	R.H.C.
	2/9/18		do	R.H.C.
	3/9/18		7/9/18. No1. and 2 Sections marched to Sheet 28. I.10. Central	R.H.C.
YPRES.	4/9/18		MORPETH Dump came under the orders of the C.O. of this Unit. Ammunition delivered to Battery Positions and Forward Dumps	R.H.C.
	5/9/18		Capt. E.A.PRICE, M.C. R.F.A. struck off the strength on proceeding to England, en route for NEW ZEALAND	R.H.C.
	"		Capt. J.O. GUERTIN. A.V.C. struck off the strength of this Unit.	R.H.C.
	"		Lieut. D.R. CHALMERS. A.N.C. taken on the strength of this Unit.	R.H.C.
	"		Casualties by Enemy Shell fire:- 1. OR killed, 1. OR Wounded. 3 mules killed, 1 mule Wounded.	R.H.C.
	6/9/18		Lieut. S.H. RICHMAN. U.S.M.C, attached to 2⁰⁰ Royal Irish Fusrs.	R.H.C.
	7/9/18		Ordinary Daily Routine	R.H.C.
	8/9/18		Ammunition delivered to Forward Dumps	R.H.C.
	9/9/18		do	R.H.C.
	10/9/18		do	R.H.C.
	11/9/18		do	R.H.C.
	12/9/18		do	R.H.C.
	13/9/18		do	R.H.C.
	"		Capt. F.W.H. MAGEE. R.F.A. attached to H.Qrs. 36 D.A. and Performing the duties of Acting Staff Captain.	R.H.C.
	14/9/18		2⁰⁰ Lieut. A. SIMMONS. R.F.A. Assumes the duties of Acting Adjutant of this Unit.	R.H.C.
	"		S.A.A. Section marched to BECELAERE Area.	R.H.C.
	"		No1. No1. and 2. Sections marched to DADIZEELE Area.	R.H.C.
	"		ASHMORE Dump came under orders of the CO. of this Unit.	R.H.C.

Army Form C. 2118.

WAR DIARY
or
INTELLIGENCE SUMMARY.
(Erase heading not required.)

Instructions regarding War Diaries and Intelligence Summaries are contained in F. S. Regs., Part II. and the Staff Manual respectively. Title pages will be prepared in manuscript.

Place	Date	Hour	Summary of Events and Information	Remarks and references to Appendices
DADIZEELE	15/10		Ammunition delivered to Battery Wagon Lines of 153 & 173 Bde R.F.A.	R.H.C.
	16/10		MORPETH Dump closed	R.H.C.
	"		Ashnow Dump handed over to 41st D.A.	R.H.C.
	17/10		Ordinary Daily Routine	R.H.C.
	18/10		2nd Lt. F.E. LEVI. R.F.A. struck off the strength on posting to 153 Bde R.F.A.	R.H.C.
	"		No 1. and 2 Sections marched to LENDELEEDE Area	R.H.C.
	"		Dump formed at Sheet 29/B.14.d.	R.H.C.
LENDELEEDE	"		Ammunition delivered to Batteries of 153 & 173 Bde R.F.A	R.H.C.
	19/10		S.A.A. Section marched to LENDELEEDE Area	R.H.C.
	"		Capt. R.F.T. COLSELL R.F.A. assumed command of this Unit vice F.G.T.H.C. Bleu, 189 Birmingham San. R.H.C.	R.H.C.
	"		Ammunition delivered to 153 & 173 Bdes RFA also D.T.M.O.	R.H.C.
	20/10		Ordinary Daily Routine	R.H.C.
	21/10		No. 1 and 2 Sections marched to Sheet 29/B.15.a.o.5.	R.H.C.
	"		Ammunition delivered to forward dumps during today at Shet 29/C.24.d.	R.H.C.
	"		Capt. F.I. COTCHING R.F.A. posted from 153 Bde R.F.A. & assumed No. 1 Section with effect from 18/10.	R.H.C.
	22/10		Ordinary Daily Routine.	R.H.C.
	23/10		do	R.H.C.
	24/10		No. 1 Section 29 K S.A.C. came under orders of the C.O. of this Unit.	R.H.C.
	25/10		No. 9, No. 1 and 2 Sections marched to BEVERN Area	R.H.C.
	"		S.A.A. Section marched to Sheet 29/B.15.c.3.0	R.H.C.
BEVERN	26/10		Ammunition collected from the Battery Positions	R.H.C.
	27/10		C.26.d. A.R.P. handed over to 34th D.A.	R.H.C.
	"		No. 1 Section 29 K D.A.C. ceased to be purchases by C.O. of this Unit	R.H.C.

WAR DIARY
or
INTELLIGENCE SUMMARY.

Army Form C. 2118.

(Erase heading not required.)

Place	Date	Hour	Summary of Events and Information	Remarks and references to Appendices
BEVERN LAVVE	27/10		No.1 and No.2 Sections marched to LAVVE area.	R.H.C.
	28/10		S.A.A. Section marched to LAVVE area	R.H.C.
	29/10		Ordinary Daily Routine	R.H.C.
	30/10		do	R.H.C.
	31/10		do	R.H.C.
			OFFICERS. O.R.s ANIMALS	R.H.C.
			Total Casualties during month — NIL. KILLED 1. WOUNDED 1. KILLED 3 WOUNDED 1.	R.H.C.

31/10/18.

Robt F.J. Cobell
Captain R.I.C.
Commanding 36th Divisional Ammunition Column

Army Form C. 2118.

36 D Am Col 35

WAR DIARY
or
INTELLIGENCE SUMMARY.
(Erase heading not required.)

Place	Date	Hour	Summary of Events and Information	Remarks and references to Appendices
LAUWE	1/8		Ordinary Daily Routine.	AHR
	2/8		Inspection of this Unit by Commander X'th Corps.	AHR
	3/8		Capt: F.W.H. MAGEE. R.F.A. rejoins from H.Qrs. 36th D.A.	AHR
			2nd Lt. J.C.CHRISTIE. R.F.A. posted to 173 @Bde R.F.A. and struck off the strength of this unit.	AHR
			2nd Lt. P.CALLENDER. R.F.A. posted to 153 @Bde R.F.A. do	AHR
			Lieut. J.C.CLAYTON-HARDIE. R.F.A. taken on the strength of this unit from 173 @Bde R.F.A.	AHR
			Lieut. R.D.FORSTER. R.F.A. taken on the strength of this unit from 153 @Bde R.F.A.	AHR
			2nd Lt. J. WILLIAMS. R.F.A. do	AHR
MARCKE.	4/8		H.Qrs. and No. 2. Section marched to MARCKE Area	AHR
	5/8		Lt. Col. J.H.G. RILEY. R.F.A. rejoins from Leave and assumes Command of this Unit.	AHR
	6/8		Ordinary Daily Routine.	AHR
	7/8		do	AHR
	8/8		do	AHR
			Lieut. W.R.PICKETT. R.F.A. posted from No.1. Section to No.2. Section	AHR
			Lt. E.B.BRADFORD. R.F.A. " " 2 " " 1 "	AHR
			Lt. H.BROWNING. R.F.A. taken on the strength of this Unit from R.F.A. Base Depot.	AHR
	9/8		Ordinary Daily Routine.	AHR
	10/8		do	AHR
	11/8		do	AHR
	12/8		H.Qrs. No.1. 2. and 3.R.A. Section marches to TOURCOING.	AHR
TOURCOING	13/8		Ordinary Daily Routine.	AHR

Army Form C. 2118.

WAR DIARY
or
INTELLIGENCE SUMMARY.
(Erase heading not required.)

Instructions regarding War Diaries and Intelligence Summaries are contained in F. S. Regs., Part II. and the Staff Manual respectively. Title pages will be prepared in manuscript.

Place	Date	Hour	Summary of Events and Information	Remarks and references to Appendices
TOURCOING	14/4/18		Ordinary Daily Routine	AA
	15/4/18		do	AA
	16/4/18		do	AA
	17/4/18		do	AA
	18/4/18		do	AA
	19/4/18		do	AA
	20/4/18		Capt. A.W. Thomson. M.C. U.S.M.C. taken on the strength of the Unit.	AA
	21/4/18		Ordinary Daily Routine.	AA
	22/4/18		do	AA
	23/4/18		do	AA
	24/4/18		do	AA
	25/4/18		do	AA
	26/4/18		do	AA
	27/4/18		do	AA
	28/4/18		do	AA
	29/4/18		do	AA
	30/4/18		do	AA
			Total Casualties to Eventual & Animals — Nil.	
	1/5/18			

A.Wiley Lieut RFA
Comdg 36" Divnl Amm Comp

WAR DIARY
or
INTELLIGENCE SUMMARY.

Army Form C. 2118.

36 D Am Col

Vol 36

Place	Date	Hour	Summary of Events and Information	Remarks and references to Appendices
TOURCOING	1/7/8		Ordinary Daily Routine.	
	2/7/8		do	
	3/7/8		do	
	4/7/8		do	
	5/7/8		do	
	6/7/8		do	
	7/7/8		do	
	8/7/8		do	
	9/7/8		do	
	10/7/8		do	
	11/7/8		Capt. A.W. Thomson. U.S.M.C. to England, struck off the strength	
	12/7/8		Ordinary Daily Routine	
	13/7/8		do	
	14/7/8		do	
	15/7/8		do	
	16/7/8		do	
	17/7/8		do	
	18/7/8		do	
	19/7/8		do	
	20/7/8		2nd Lt. H. Marsh. R.F.A. taken on the strength of the Unit from 17/7/18	

Army Form C. 2118.

WAR DIARY
or
INTELLIGENCE SUMMARY.
(Erase heading not required.)

Place	Date	Hour	Summary of Events and Information	Remarks and references to Appendices
TOURCOING.	21/12/18		Ordinary Daily Routine	A.R.
	22/12/18		do	A.R.
	23/12/18		Lieut E.B. BRADFORD. R.F.A. 3 Englands struck off the strength with effect	A.R.
	24/12/18		Ordinary Daily Routine	A.R.
	25/12/18		do	A.R.
	26/12/18		do	A.R.
	27/12/18		do	A.R.
	28/12/18		do	A.R.
	29/12/18		do	A.R.
	30/12/18		do	A.R.
	31/12/18		do	A.R.
			Casualties to Personnel & Animals during the month :- Nil.	
	31/12/18			

H. Riley Major R.F.A.
Comdg 36th Divnl Ammn Colmn.

R.A.C.

WAR DIARY
or
INTELLIGENCE SUMMARY.
(Erase heading not required.)

Army Form C. 2118.

36 D Au Cd
Vol 37

Place	Date	Hour	Summary of Events and Information	Remarks and references to Appendices
TOURCOING	1/9		Ordinary Daily Routine.	
	2/9		do	
	3/9		do	
	4/9		Major J.H.G. RILES, RFA and Capt. C. WILLIAMSON, RFA mentioned in Dispatches	
	5/9		Ordinary Daily Routine.	
	6/9		do	
	7/9		do	
	8/9		do	
	9/9		2nd Lt. J. H. WILLIAMS R.F.A. awarded the Military Cross. Capt. R. T. COLSELL R.F.A. of England struck off the strength.	
	10/9		Lt. H. BROWNING. R.F.A. posted to II Corps and struck off the strength. Lt. W. R. PICKETT. R.F.A. to command No. 2. Section and wear to Reduce of its rank. Capt. Lt. J. CLAYTON HARDIE R.F.A. of England. struck off the strength.	
	11/9		Lt. Col. J.H.G. RILES. R.F.A. & Capt. F.W.H. MAGEE. R.F.A. awarded the Belgian CROIX DE GUERRE.	
	12/9		Ordinary Daily Routine.	
	13/9		do	
	14/9		do	
	15/9		do	
	16/9		do	
	17/9		do	
	18/9		do	
	19/9		do	

Army Form C. 2118.

WAR DIARY
or
INTELLIGENCE SUMMARY.
(Erase heading not required.)

Instructions regarding War Diaries and Intelligence Summaries are contained in F. S. Regs., Part II. and the Staff Manual respectively. Title pages will be prepared in manuscript.

Place	Date	Hour	Summary of Events and Information	Remarks and references to Appendices
TOURCOING	20/9		Lt A. STILWELL R.F.A. Posted as Second in Command of B/158 Bde & to wear the insignia of the rank of Captain whilst so employed	A.H.R
	20/9		2Lt J.C. CHRISTIE, R.F.A. posted from 173@Bde & taken on the strength of No.1. Section	A.H.R
	21/9		Ordinary Daily Routine	A.H.R
	22/9		do	A.H.R
	23/9		do	A.H.R
	24/9		do	A.H.R
	25/9		Lieut A. SIMMONS R.F.A. to England. Struck off the strength	A.H.R
	26/9		Ordinary Daily Routine	A.H.R
	27/9		do	A.H.R
	28/9		do	A.H.R
	29/9		do	A.H.R
	30/9		do	A.H.R
			Casualties to Personnel & Animals during the month :- Nil.	A.H.R

1/7/19.

A. Wilcot
Col. R.F.A.
Commanding 158th Bde.
Army of Occupation

Army Form C. 2118.

WAR DIARY
or
INTELLIGENCE SUMMARY.
(Erase heading not required.)

Instructions regarding War Diaries and Intelligence Summaries are contained in F. S. Regs., Part II. and the Staff Manual respectively. Title pages will be prepared in manuscript.

Place	Date	Hour	Summary of Events and Information	Remarks and references to Appendices
TOURCOING	1/1/19		Ordinary Daily Routine.	
	2/1/19		Lt. R.D. FORSTER R.F.A. Struck off the strength with effect from 26-1-19.	
	3/1/19		Ordinary Daily Routine.	
	4/1/19		do	
	5/1/19		do	
	6/1/19		do	
	7/1/19		do	
	8/1/19		do	
	9/1/19		do	
	10/1/19		do	
	11/1/19		do	
	12/1/19		do	
	13/1/19		do	
	14/1/19		Rev. R.C.H.G. ELLIOTT C.F. struck off the strength with effect from today's date	
	15/1/19		Rev. A.W. BARTON C.F. taken on the strength of this Unit.	
	16/1/19		Ordinary Daily Routine	
	17/1/19		do	
	18/1/19		do	

Army Form C. 2118.

WAR DIARY
or
INTELLIGENCE SUMMARY.

(Erase heading not required.)

Instructions regarding War Diaries and Intelligence Summaries are contained in F. S. Regs., Part II. and the Staff Manual respectively. Title pages will be prepared in manuscript.

Place	Date	Hour	Summary of Events and Information	Remarks and references to Appendices
TOURCOING	19/7/9		Ordinary Daily Routine	
	20/7/9		do	
	21/7/9		do	
	22/7/9		do	
	23/7/9		do	
	24/7/9		do	
	25/7/9		do	
	26/7/9		do	
	27/7/9		do	
	28/7/9		Casualties to Personnel & Animals during the Month :- Nil	

28/7/9.

J.A. Mager Capt. R.I.t
Officer Commanding, 36 "Division Amm Column

www.ingramcontent.com/pod-product-compliance
Lightning Source LLC
Chambersburg PA
CBHW081552160426
43191CB00011B/1905